STAY OUT

—— *of* ——

REAL ESTATE
JAIL

BARBARA BELL-OLSEN

STAY OUT

——————— *of* ———————

REAL ESTATE

J**A**IL

YOUR LIFELINE TO REAL ESTATE

iUniverse LLC
Bloomington

STAY OUT OF REAL ESTATE JAIL
YOUR LIFELINE TO REAL ESTATE

iUniverse books may be ordered through booksellers or by contacting:

iUniverse
1663 Liberty Drive
Bloomington, IN 47403
www.iuniverse.com
1-800-Authors (1-800-288-4677)

ISBN: 978-1-4759-9203-8 (sc)
ISBN: 978-1-4759-9204-5 (e)

Library of Congress Control Number: 2013909654

Printed in the United States of America

iUniverse rev. date: 7/15/2013

To Anthony G. Andrews

Tony is a marvellous man who supported me emotionally, offering his opinion and advice. Without his encouragement, understanding and sense of humour, this book would never have been completed. He sparked the creative side in me, and he encouraged me to keep going until it was finished. He genuinely believed in me.

It has taken me over three and a half years to write this book and set up my website, www.barbarabellolsen.com, so that you can access everything reviewed in the book plus many more in-depth topics by downloading word-processing files. I kept on telling Tony that it really was a good thing I had no life, but it was a shame that I inflicted that lifestyle on him too. He was always there for me.

I am very lucky Tony remained supportive and backed me 100 percent, although there were many times he asked me to disengage from the computer. He truly thought—and rightly so—that I had grown attached (literally) to this machine. He did have a problem one night when the computer joined us in the bedroom, but that didn't happen again.

I definitely have been missing in action for a very long time, but he was very supportive. He attended many a dinner and weekend outing without me since I was too busy editing my material. He also prepared an awful lot of meals for both of us, which I really appreciate.

I also sincerely thank my family, my friends, my colleagues and everyone who helped make this book possible. Just to let you know, I am now available to have a life and meet for coffee anytime.

I also dedicate this book to those real estate professionals who have provided ethical and outstanding service to their clients and customers and to those who are not even aware how remarkable the profession they have joined is.

I thank all my students who have taken my courses over the years and those who will be joining me in the future. You are an amazing group of people who have inspired me by asking me to help you. Now I am fulfilling my dream of doing just that. I am privileged and honoured to give back to my industry, and I thank you for your encouragement and for telling me to "Hurry up and publish the book!"

My students and colleagues know I am useless on the computer, so I must thank iUniverse for all their help in editing and publishing *Stay Out of Real Estate Jail*. They added their wisdom and professional talents to lift the book above the standards I could have achieved if I'd just gone ahead and published it on my own.

CONTENTS

FOREWORD

by Jeff Scouten, Partner, Henshall Scouten

Real estate agents sail in treacherous waters. The professional rules and practice standards governing you are demanding and continually changing, the hours are long, the deadlines are hard, the clients are anxious and stressed and the consequences of screwing up—professionally and financially—can be huge. Treacherous rocks also lurk all around you just below the surface: an innocuous-looking charge on title with drastic implications for the client, a glitch in securing financing, a quirky provision in the strata bylaws, a nonconforming use, an encroaching structure, a buried oil tank, rodents in the attic ... and so the list goes on (and on). Add to the mix the pressures and vagaries of changing market conditions, with parties looking for ways out of contracts you've worked hard to put together, and you have a recipe for a shipwreck just waiting to happen. As the professional on the prow of the ship, you are cannon fodder for the anger and blame of disappointed clients when things go wrong, whether you deserve it or not.

Stay Out of Real Estate Jail is the loving creation and culmination of years of thought and effort on the part of Barbara Bell-Olsen. Barb is a leader in the area of professional education and has been at the forefront in the development of "best practices" in the real estate industry in British Columbia. Since she received her license in 1979, Barb's career in real estate has spanned the full spectrum of roles in the field. In her early years, she was a top producer with the Permanent and with Montreal Trust, so she well understands the day-to-day challenges involved in frontline sales. In 1994 she purchased her own business, Coldwell Banker Bell-Olsen Realty, which she operated for six years. Since 2000, Barb has been the managing broker for Royal LePage Westside in Vancouver. She comes to the task of writing a book like this knowing the business of real estate inside out and from all angles.

Barb has a keen passion for professional education in her chosen field. Over the past 20 years or more, she has presented or sponsored countless courses, seminars and training sessions for REALTORS®. She has written and taught five courses on contract writing that have been approved by the British Columbia Real Estate Association for credit as a part of the province's Professional Development Program (PDP). She has written interview questionnaires to assist managing brokers in offices across the country in recruiting new members to their sales teams. Her name and trademark lively and personal writing style are already known to many in the profession through the entertaining and informative newsletters she has put out over the years, *Bell-Olsen's Best* and, more recently, *Barb's Buzz on Business*.

This book, like all of the fruits of Barb's mind and talents, is a true labour of love. Barb considers real estate to be more than a business or vocation. She sees it as a noble profession, requiring high skill and integrity on the part of its members, that plays an important role in society and touches the lives of clients in important ways. She is proud of her profession and is one of its fiercest defenders and most ardent cheerleaders. She also cares deeply—almost to a maternal degree—for members of the profession who happen to come under her wing as a managing broker, teacher or mentor. In my many years as a practicing lawyer bumping up against the real estate industry, I have never met anyone quite like her. She is a force of nature.

Barb has summoned all of her knowledge, passion and experience and skillfully brought them to bear in creating this remarkable book. It is chock-full of guidance on day-to-day issues and perils you're bound to encounter, with practical tips and precedents that will not only steer you through the rocks but also save you a huge amount of time and get you home earlier at night. A wealth of further material—forms, checklists, sample letters and contract clauses—in editable form customizable to your specific needs is also available through her website, www.barbarabellolsen.com.

For those hoping to make a living and sleep at night while plying the dangerous waters of the real estate world, this book is your *Mariner's Handbook*. Just as that book must by law be carried on all UK seagoing passenger vessels, so this one should be required reading and a regular reference guide for you as REALTORS® in navigating past the hazards inherent in your practice through to happy shores for yourselves and your clients.

Jeff Scouten is a founding partner of the Vancouver law firm of Henshall Scouten. He has been a lawyer for almost 30 years and regularly represents REALTORS®, brokerages and other clients on matters relating to real estate, including professional discipline matters, commission disputes, transactional matters and contract disputes arising from residential and commercial real estate transactions.

PREFACE

I have been in the real estate industry for over 34 years, and I can truthfully say that not a day of it has been work. I love this industry, and I am fiercely proud to say I am a real estate agent. I have wanted to publish this book for years to give something back to a profession that has done nothing but give me the opportunity to have a wonderful career and life.

I have obtained all my licensing requirements including the certificate for attending the Industrial, Commercial and Investment (ICI) courses.

I have presented numerous courses, seminars and training regarding industry standards, ethics and contracts. I have consulted, trained and educated one on one, in group settings and in very large seminars or conferences.

I wrote interview questionnaires to assist managing brokers across Canada in hiring and retaining new and experienced real estate agents. I also wrote and presented seminars on cross-selling between a financial institute and real estate brokerage. These policies and procedures were implemented and distributed between these two specific firms across Canada.

When Canada Trust merged with Coldwell Banker Affiliates of Canada, I purchased the office Coldwell Banker Bell-Olsen Realty and built my own (heritage) "boutique style" office building.

I created a training session called "Legal Pursuit" that contained questions and answers about our industry standards, ethics, rules, regulations, values, writing contracts, etc., and I produced, edited and published (with help from my salespeople) *Bell-Olsen's Best: Your Guide to Real Estate,* a monthly newspaper for the public.

I was flown to Toronto, Ontario, Canada, and assisted in helping set policies and improve management standards and operations for the franchise broker/owners and their staff.

In October 2000, I proudly became the managing broker for Royal LePage Westside. One accomplishment I am quite thrilled of is the fact that all of my sales agents followed me to the new brokerage.

I write and teach courses—including four levels of "Writing Enforceable Contracts" and a full-day course called "Multiple Offers"—as an outside approved accredited instructor for our British Columbia Real Estate Association. This all started in January 2005 when British Columbia brought in the Real Estate Services Act (RESA) and the Real Estate Development Marketing Act (REDMA).

I had already been writing my courses for both new and experienced licensees, but I became passionate about it when I realized that the priority mandate of our authorities is to protect the public. I wondered who is protecting us as real estate agents. If agents are protected, that automatically leads to the protection of the public. Not only that, in order to keep our license, we must comply with everything no matter what we think about the rules and regulations.

After writing my student manuals and teaching my colleagues, I found that one of the biggest concerns is that we all have great intentions of reading the information from our authorities, but half the time we just don't get to it. That led to the introduction of *Barb's Buzz on Business*, a free newsletter with updates on changes and confirmation of industry-related recommendations and/or warnings. I will often recap in easy-to-understand language the concerns that have arisen.

Often I act as an intermediary between my students and our authorities. When our agents have questions, they normally send them to me and I forward their concerns. This saves our authorities from receiving numerous questions on the same topic. I sincerely thank our authorities and our associations, including their executive officers and all their staff. They always offer their assistance and advice, and they do it with speed.

I thrive on the energy of people and being able to help them better themselves. I became passionate about sharing my real estate knowledge with you and want to help make your writing of a Contract of Purchase and Sale so simple that you would be proud to show it on television or to the world. Think about the last contract you prepared. Would you be happy to have it reviewed by your authorities or displayed on the Internet for everyone to see? If not, then when you implement the plans and checklists I am going to share with you, I will ask you this question again. I bet you will be thrilled to have any of your contracts in the spotlight.

It is fantastic to show you just how easily you can run your business and increase your income, all the while being assured and confident in what you are doing. Wouldn't it be great if you could triple or quadruple your income without any extra effort? If you follow the suggestions here, including the prepared clauses and phrases, you are on your way, and your bank account will absolutely explode.

I am a real estate agent, and I have experienced almost every aspect of the industry, so

I am one of you who will most likely purchase this book. I have been in the trenches, believe me. Some of the situations I faced are described later in the book.

I personally know how hard a real estate agent works and how much time and money you invest in each and every transaction, but you must have a paper trail in place to be able to prove what you discussed, reviewed and suggested to your clients. The paper-trail requirements also inspired me to share my knowledge and experience with you. There are far too many discipline cases by our authorities, and most of them are absolutely unnecessary if an agent just took a little more care and had a plan of action. You must have procedures in place, which I will show you when we get to the nuts and bolts of writing the Contract of Purchase and Sale.

This book is directed mainly at writing a Contract of Purchase and Sale with buyers who are in an offer situation where there are no other competing offers—a one-on-one situation, not a multiple-offer situation. You are not in competition and have the luxury of adding in all the clauses and phrases that will safeguard and protect the interests of your buyers.

I want to revise the inner workings of real estate so that you are increasing your volume of business while implementing new methods, including having a paperless operation if you so choose. I want to give you unique and modern procedures and urge you to always follow the same ones every time you meet a new client or prepare an offer. You must be consistent. It is critical.

The fresh approach I am going to share with you removes any fear, apprehension or nervousness when you are ready to write an offer. When the buyers are ready to write, you will be ready too. You will be amazingly relaxed and confident, and you will have a well-organized and superior blueprint to follow to accomplish this. Your Contract of Purchase and Sale will be extraordinary and protect all parties to the transaction.

Once you personally own all the documents, checklists and statements, you will be the creator of the most notable and respected contracts. Your clients will rightly realize that you're an exceptional professional who is protecting them each and every step of the way through the entire buying process.

I will take you through the purchasing process and explain in detail each of these proven methods so you can educate your buyers to the fullest and remove any anxiety or apprehension they may have. They will be so impressed with your expertise they will spread the word to everyone they know, and that will lead to more business for you.

You will assist all other agents, which again will help build your career with more co-operation from your colleagues. They will know that when you present an offer, you are more than capable, you are a pleasure to work with, and more importantly, they won't have to rewrite the wording in your contracts. Your contracts are well-organized and accurate, and you are known to be precise and efficient. They will tell others just how enjoyable it was to work with you on a transaction.

You will be building relationships with the public and with your colleagues. It is a win-win situation for all, but especially for you.

If you follow the guidelines in this book and on my website at www.barbarabellolsen.com, your career will skyrocket, and you will be amazed and excited by the positive changes you will face. You will wonder what you have been doing all these years—or, if you are new, you will realize just how easy and profitable your career in real estate can be.

I sincerely believe that a real estate agent is in a very high position of trust and the public and our colleagues rely on our competence, expertise, co-operation, professionalism and integrity, and we must convey these traits at all times. We need to earn this trust. We deserve this trust, but we must constantly display these skills and traits in our everyday lives and business. We must "walk the talk."

By following and implementing the statements, subjects and property specifics I am going to share with you, you will earn and deserve the trust and faith everyone has in you. You are protecting the public, your colleagues and yourself. You are perfecting your skills and abilities. What a wonderful profession you have chosen. What more could any of us ever want?

The information and suggestions I am going to reveal and share with you will remove any apprehension you may have. It will save you time, trouble and hassle; it will save you money; and in fact it will help you make more money.

[Note: Throughout the book, where the word "agent" is used, it also could read "representative" or "rep" and/or "licensee." This is the same with the word "client" and/or "customer." A client is someone you have an agency relationship with, and a customer is someone you may have no agency relationship with. I have limited the use to one or the other words above only for the simplicity of reading.]

ACKNOWLEDGEMENTS

A sincere thank-you to *all* the real estate professional associations, boards, councils, institutes, etc., and those below for the information they have available for all of us as professional real estate agents.

B. C. Assessment

B. C. Government

B. C. Northern Real Estate Board

B. C. Real Estate Association (BCREA)

B. C. Real Estate Guide CCH Canadian Ltd.

B. C. Securities Commission

Blaney, Mike The Marketing Guy (Website)

Brokerage Standards Manual

Budget Printing, Calvin Jang

Building Owners & Managers Association (BOMA BC)

Bury, Andrew Partner, Gowlings Barristers and Solicitors

Canada Customs and Revenue Agency

Canada Mortgage and Housing Corporation

Canadian Real Estate Association

Canadian Regulators Group

Chilliwack Real Estate Board

City of Vancouver

Code of Ethics

Competition Act

Do Not Call

Financial Institutions Commission

Fraser Valley Real Estate Board

Gioventu, Tony, Executive Director of the Condominium

Home Owners' Association of B.C. (CHOA)

Government of British Columbia

Government of Canada

Heritage Branch BC—Heritage Trust

Heritage Conservation

Homeowner Protection Act

South Okanagan Real Estate Board
Vancouver Island Real Estate Board
Victoria Real Estate Board
WEBForms™

Also, a very sincere and personal thank-you to:

Jeffrey P. Scouten, barrister and solicitor, Henshall Scouten, for all his outstanding advice, suggestions, consultations, and incredible wisdom and caring for all our licensees.

Stewart Henderson, Macdonald Realty 1st Pioneer; Jim McCaughan, Landmark Realty Corp.; Kelvin Neufeld, Sutton-Premier Realty; and Scott Olson, Macdonald Realty Olympic, for all their support and encouragement and also for taking the time to discuss a number of issues and concerns in our industry with me.

David Metcalf, my very special friend, who I sincerely thank for all his words of wisdom, his encouragement and his belief in me. *"What can go wrong?"*

David Moore, Director, the University of British Columbia, Sauder Business School, and the Real Estate Council of B. C., British Columbia Real Estate Association, Errors and Omissions Insurance, all real estate boards, and all other industry members, advisors and colleagues for their assistance.

Robert Laing, Chief Executive Officer, and the British Columbia Real Estate Association (BCREA) for their guidance and information.

Robert Fawcett, Executive Officer; Larry Buttress, Deputy Executive Officer; David Berger, Director, Legal Services; and the Real Estate Council of British Columbia for taking the time to answer my many questions and e-mails.

Kim Spencer, Manager of Professional Standards, REBGV, for taking the time to review and discuss clauses and the Real Estate Services Act information, and for answering numerous questions.

Brian E. Taylor Associate Counsel, Local Government who is a partner at Bull, Housser & Tupper and M. M. (Mike) Mangan, B.Comm., LL.B. for all their contribution and dedicated service to our profession.

Bill Binnie, Royal LePage Northshore, City Centre & Sunshine Coast, and Chris Simmons, Royal LePage Westside, City Centre & Sunshine Coast, for allowing me to present my courses to their licensees.

The Fraser Valley Real Estate Board, for being the first board to allow me the opportunity to present "Writing Enforceable Contracts" to help all real estate agents write enforceable contracts in order to protect themselves and the public (Kelvin Neufeld, Scott Olson and Denise Johnson, Manager, Education, Fraser Valley Real Estate Board).

The Chilliwack and District Real Estate Board, the Fraser Valley Real Estate Board, the Real Estate Board of Greater Vancouver, the South Okanagan Real Estate Board, the Vancouver Island Real Estate Board, and the Victoria Real Estate Board for offering my seminars to all licensees.

All our authorities and associations, including our executive officers and all their staff.

Thank you all very much. You are amazing!

Barb

Disclaimer—Caveat

The information, commentary and precedents contained in this text and any sample clauses, phrases, statements, subjects and the like are provided for general informational and educational purposes only and do not constitute legal advice. The author, although an experienced real estate professional, is not a lawyer, and the contents of this text should not be construed as legal advice to be applied to any specific factual situation. Readers unsure of their responsibilities in particular situations should in all cases consult with their managing broker, their authorities and/or a lawyer for guidance.

Although the author has made every effort to ensure that the information contained herein is accurate and current, the author, publisher and any contributors, including all those acknowledged and thanked, cannot and do not guarantee that the information is either. Before acting on information contained in this book and the accompanying manual and website, readers should always consult and rely on primary sources—including government resources and information published by their relevant governing bodies—when determining the laws, rules or professional standards that pertain to particular situations. The statutes, regulations, case law and professional rules governing the provision of real estate services are also subject to continual change and vary significantly from one jurisdiction to another. The application of law to specific circumstances can also vary widely depending on the facts of any individual case.

For these reasons, the author and publisher strongly recommend that readers, whenever in any doubt as to their professional responsibilities, consult with their managing broker, authorities and/or with a lawyer when advising clients, making decisions and preparing documents for use in particular situations. The author and publisher and any contributors, including all those acknowledged and thanked, do not accept any liability for reliance by readers on the information, commentary or precedents contained in this book.

Legal Disclaimer from Barb

Even if I was a lawyer, which I am not, there is absolutely no way I could cover all the legalities for each state, province or other area where you may live and practise real estate. There are too many different rules and regulations.

However, according to my research and help from lawyers and judges, our regulations are very similar, and you should be able to adapt the wording to suit your authorities' requirements. What I am giving you is what I have seen and/or experienced as a salesperson, broker/owner, managing broker and instructor.

Please verify these items including all forms with your own legal/professional people and the authorities and legislation in your market area. I don't want you to misinterpret anything covered in any of the material.

CHAPTER 1
STAY OUT OF REAL ESTATE JAIL

Congratulations on purchasing *Stay Out of Real Estate Jail*. Between this book and the information you can own and download from my website at www.barbarabellolsen.com you are going to be able to jumpstart your terrific career in real estate—or, if you are a seasoned pro, you are going to be able to rejuvenate, refresh and build on what you have already accomplished. Your business will explode, as will your bank account.

If you are anything like me, you have started reading this book on this page and omitted reading the foreword, the preface and the disclaimer. I strongly urge you to go back and start by reviewing the information in front of this chapter. The editors who have helped me rework this book numerous times suggest storytelling should be in a specific order. That means there is information in the previous sections that will help you understand why some items and ideas are presented in a specific style or order. I always jump to the meat and potatoes, but I now realize the importance of starting right at the beginning of the book.

You will see that I have been successful, become a nominee, bought my own franchise and built my own "boutique style" office building in Vancouver, British Columbia, Canada. I am presently a managing broker for a large Canadian franchise brokerage, and I write and teach courses—including four levels of "Writing Enforceable Contracts" and a full-day course called "Multiple Offers"—as an outside approved accredited instructor for our British Columbia Real Estate Association.

Most people have a hobby. It could be fishing, hunting, boating, cooking, arts and crafts, or many other wonderful interests. I love cooking and trying out new recipes, but I seem to have a passion for the real estate profession that keeps on growing. My mind must be a bit weird, because I love the intricacies of our industry. I have a knack for it, and the information seems to stay in my brain. I often tell my students that I have no life. I enjoy and thrive on how to better improve our profession, how to improve our image and more importantly, how to help my fellow colleagues.

It has almost become an obsession with me, to the point that I believed it was time to put pen to paper and share my knowledge with those who truly want to become the crème de la crème. This book and my website were over three and a half years in the making, but now it is closer to four years. I was so used to teaching and being able to verbally explain my written material that I honestly had trouble writing this, because I kept forgetting I won't be personally reviewing it with you.

That's where the editors were of huge help in having me reorganize and re-edit everything a number of times. They showed me that I must be explicit and definitive in what the procedures and methods are, and I need to remember we won't be chit-chatting about the particular subject. If ever you have questions or concerns, you are more than welcome to e-mail me at barbarabellolsen@shaw.ca, and I will try to be of assistance. I am just so very lucky that I can now share my methods and information with you.

There are not very many agents who want to be a managing broker. For one, the pay is nowhere near what you make by selling real estate, and the job is that of looking after the agents in your brokerage. I personally love it.

Managing brokers are given the authority and information to make decisions in a timely manner and oversee the brokerage operations and those of their agents. They ensure that the brokerage business is carried out competently and in accordance with the Act, regulations, rules and bylaws, and also ensure that there is an adequate level of supervision for agents and for employees and others who perform duties on behalf of the brokerage.

When my agents don't understand something or need some help, I will do everything I can to assist them. When I have to think outside the box to help them, I really thrive on that. There is almost always a solution, and together we will work through the problem and solve it. It is so great to be able to help.

I get to assist with educating both our new agents and our experienced agents, and I am responsible for reviewing their contracts and making sure they are current with the rules and regulations. As part of my duties, I send a note about any errors or items that may become of concern in the future so that they are up to date and know for the next time. I hate doing this, but it is part of my managing broker requirements, and my salespeople know I am only trying to help them for another contract they may prepare that may have the same items or concerns. Thank goodness they understand and don't take it personally, knowing it is what is required of me.

This is the perfect career stage for me. As I said earlier, I have never worked a day in my life since entering real estate, and I absolutely love working with sales agents and people and being able to help them.

That too led to this book. It was time to reveal and share everything I have ever learned with the world. Why not? There is absolutely no sense in all this valuable information staying locked in my brain. I want to help make you the best you can be, and it is so very easy if you follow the proven methods I am going to recommend you utilize. I am going to give you the best support system and explain how to put a Contract of Purchase and Sale together without really having to think about it. Everything is also available on my website so you can own and download a word-processing file and copy and paste what you need after editing the statements, subjects, property specifics and the like.

When you are writing a Contract of Purchase and Sale, your life can be easy, but you need checklists and forms to make it that way. The public will be so impressed by your thoroughness and your professional, ethical and careful attention to detail that they will be thrilled to have you as their real estate agent. They will feel safe. They will know what to expect because you walked them through the entire process. They will know you care and are protecting them.

Often, agents can get scared or frightened when asked to write a contract. You may worry that you'll mess it up, and that is one of the main reasons for problems in our industry. It is so easy to forget something, or you go too fast or sometimes get a little overwhelmed preparing the contract. It can be nerve-racking. Some have told me they are almost paralyzed when it is time to write the contract. You want to protect the public and yourself.

With the help I'll give you in this book, you won't have to experience that dreaded feeling in your gut when you're asked to prepare a contract. You won't question what you have to do and what statements, clauses and subjects to use. You will have so much knowledge, confidence and skill that you will easily take your clients to the successful closing of their purchase or sale, and you will retain them for life. Your business will soar to any level you want. How successful do you want to be? It is up to you after you read and implement the following superior structured procedures into your everyday business plan.

Whether you are new to our industry or a seasoned professional, you can do and be anything you set your mind to if you implement the timesaving, unique and inspiring concepts offered in this book.

CHAPTER 2
LEARN YOUR CRAFT

Pilots do not set out on a flight course without first following their checklists and procedures and verifying that they have done everything perfectly. They cannot afford to forget something and thank goodness for that.

You have chosen to specialize in an ever-changing profession. There is so much to remember that you need checklists and forms to make it easier. This includes predone Contracts of Purchase and Sale and addendums with all the required wording prepared and ready to go.

If you do not take the time to learn your craft and continually upgrade and educate yourself, you could run into problems by making mistakes. It is easy to do with all the disclosure requirements and the introduction of new legislation. Real estate is a very serious business, but you can have so much fun and success if you are organized, know what you are doing and have your own business plan incorporating the simple methods introduced here.

You will be someone who is proud, confident and excited while being ethical, professional and knowledgeable. Obviously, this means you will be thrilled with the contracts you prepare, and your business will grow with satisfied and happy clients who will tell everyone how great you are. Your bank account will begin increasing by leaps and bounds. It's perfect, and it is all up to you. What more could anyone want?

It would be pretty dangerous if a pilot didn't use his checklists and procedures, and it is the same for us. So let's make our professional occupation one of perfection and work together, all the while protecting our clients and customers.

Real Estate Jail—Fact or Fiction?

Fiction—we do not have a "real estate jail" per se, but we do have to face our authorities at different levels if there is ever a complaint filed against us. It is not a pleasant experience.

I should have faced our authorities when I started, but I was just plain lucky that no one complained. We have reports and newsletters we all receive from our authorities, and often there are sections of what I call *"Who's in trouble?"* Most of us read this section first to see who was has been disciplined and why.

Often these agents made a simple or stupid mistake: they went too fast, they forgot something or they were a bit careless and got caught up in the moment. They are not bad people at all. They made a mistake, which anyone can do.

Once a complaint is filed, the authorities go through each agent's contract with a fine-tooth comb looking for any and all errors that might have been made. They have the power to enforce their rules and regulations, and they often do just that. Common penalties include a fine or a license suspension for a period of time, and/or they send an agent for further education.

The shaken agents have their name published in these newsletters and often can have a "permanent mark" in their file. Who wants that to happen? No one, and as I stated, it is often something ridiculous we could have prevented had we just double-checked or taken a little more time. It is not fun at all, and it is very time-consuming preparing replies and reasons for your defence. It is stressful and just plain awful.

This book was written to help anyone this could happen to, and you will see that some of the incidents that caused a reprimand were really simple mistakes, and some were caused by failure to stay up-to-date with the requirements of our authorities and the legislation. Agents who are truly unprofessional or unethical to the detriment of the public are dealt with in a very harsh manner, and our authorities do weed out those types of people.

The authorities have a mandate to protect the public, and that means we have to do the same. So let's do it and do it right the first time. You will see how silly some of the mistakes are. With just a little more care writing the contract, adding in the statements or subjects or having more knowledge or training, there would never be a problem. Keep yourself updated and educated, and have an active plan and checklists in place for writing any type of contract. I am going to give you just such a system.

I will review in depth the primary clauses and phrases, specifically:

- the statements that could be in most contracts

- the subjects (Famous Five)

- the property specifics.

And then I will cover such items as:

- offers and counter-offers

- removing the subjects

- changing an accepted Contract of Purchase and Sale

- turning in your documents.

I will also explain how to put this all together so you never forget anything. You must focus on these items each and every time you write an offer. You cannot afford to forget anything. You must be disciplined and follow the same format with each Contract of Purchase and Sale that you write. You must be consistent. It is critical.

First I want to give you some general information, including how I ended up in the real estate industry. I will include my first few days in the profession and what happened to me with my first buyer and my first seller. This will just reinforce how things can go wrong and why, but I will then take you to an ideal order of contract writing so it never happens to you.

I will also give you a few ideas with respect to promoting yourself, advertising and a few other marketing suggestions.

CHAPTER 3
STARTING OUT

Why did I choose a career in real estate? I was working and had been working as an executive administrator to the president and vice-president of a company. The vice-president had told me for years to go into real estate because I would be so good at it. What the heck did he mean? What makes a good real estate agent?

One day he told me he was going to fire me because I was wasting my talents working for him, and I should go into real estate and work for myself. He didn't want to hear another word about it. I was devastated. *Fire me, are you kidding?* Well, he wasn't kidding. He told me he would give me one year's notice, time enough to obtain my license, and then I was gone, like it or not. What was he thinking?

He left me no choice, so off I went and took the course. I personally was forced into real estate as a profession with no idea what I was doing. I worked for these two fellows for years, and it was often six days a week and hours and hours of overtime that I didn't get paid for.

I wrote the real estate exam in a room with hundreds of other hopefuls, and I must admit I was scared to death. What if I forgot everything I learned? Although, I must be honest, in those days, the courses didn't teach me how to sell real estate at all. I just learned "stuff." It is very different today.

When I was studying for the exam, I took courses to help me pass and met a fantastic lady who became the best in our industry for a number of years. We both were extremely competitive, and I wasn't going to let her beat me on any of our assignments (we usually got the same marks). There was one area we thought might be on the exam, and we just couldn't remember all the answers.

I made up some rather rude words to remember them by, and she memorized them too. When we wrote the exam, there was that question, and I looked over to see her staring at me. We both burst out laughing. The rest of the class thought we were crazy.

I passed. Now what?

Well, the vice-president fired me as soon as he heard I passed. That was it, after all my years of dedication and service and free overtime too! I couldn't believe it. He fired me!

I was on the streets in more ways than one.

Now I had to find a brokerage to join. My classmate had already picked a company and told me there was a desk for me too. I was to be her partner. I didn't know if I wanted to do that.

She was so successful it was unbelievable, but I went to another company to learn on my own. No one told me connections and knowing people was one of the biggest assets, especially when starting out. I guess this was my first really big mistake. I should have gone with her, even if just for her connections.

She is no longer in our industry, but she was one dynamic woman. She was married to a doctor who got bored and became a lawyer, or maybe he was a lawyer and became a doctor. She was brilliant and had unbelievable connections.

One thing I did learn is that meeting people and letting everyone know what you do for a living is critical to survival in our industry. That's how you get business. Referrals and who you know. You are going to have to generate your own clientele when you first begin as a new agent, so we will cover a few promotional and advertising ideas shortly.

My First Day

I joined a large brokerage, and on my first day I was greeted by the managing broker. He showed me my desk and said, "Good luck, Barb." That was it. I waited, but nothing else happened.

My desk was sparkling clean. I could almost see my reflection. There was a phone and phone book but no pens, no paper, nothing in the drawers, nothing at all.

I saw another agent a couple of rows over at the same pristine shiny desk with just a phone and phone book too, but he had opened the phone book and was calling people.

I had nothing else to do, so I opened the phone book to a page and dialled away like crazy. They were very short conversations, since every single person said no.

That was the end of day one in the business for me. All I had to show for it was a very sore dialling finger.

My Second Day

Day two was pretty much the same; however, the support staff showed me around and told me where to find everything. They gave me the keys to the office, the alarm code and a bunch of paperwork to fill in. There were numerous people in the office, so I got to meet most of the other agents, which made me feel a bit better.

As time passed, the reality of the situation sank in. I didn't have the faintest clue of what to do, what forms to use, or even how to find a buyer or seller. Even if I did, I wouldn't know what to do with them.

I did decide—all by myself, I might add—that I should know what was on the market. That might be really important, I realized. I also knew—and again, I figured it out all by myself—that I should shout to the world that I was in real estate. That meant phoning everyone I could think of and sending notes and announcements to everyone I knew. (We didn't have e-mails back then.)

I made up a "to call" list, now referred to as a contact list, and realized it was not very long. I added in every person I could think of, including doctors, dentists, dry-cleaners, grocery-store people, car people and bank people.

Then I added in every single person from my family, including my mom and dad, friends and every acquaintance I had ever met in my life—even those from my previous job that I was fired from. I did contact them all at least once, and I knew that I had to do it again. Yes, this was fun.

I did know that I had to build relationships. It also made me feel like I was busier. I was trying to generate business. I wished I had the money to take a notice out on the front page of all the newspapers, but that was out of my range.

My Daily Routine

Eventually I got into a routine by making sure I went to the office by 9:00 a.m. at the very latest. I always diarized my day the night before, and later on, the week before. When I started, I always went on tour with my colleagues. If I didn't know the market, I really was not going to be able to help anyone.

If you are new to our industry, do not get discouraged. You need to follow the guidelines for advertising and promoting yourself. Think outside the box—who else could you let know what you do? Where could you generate business and how?

At the beginning of my new career, I did have a prioritized daily list of what to do. Did you know that they say one of the main reasons new real estate agents fail is because they were used to punching a time clock in their former jobs and having specific duties to do each and every day, and now they have all this free time and don't know what to do with it? Quite often they just don't do anything.

This can happen to seasoned agents, too, when the market changes—and believe me, it does change. I have been through some pretty rough times. Interest at 21 percent, now that was a bit of a problem. I stayed positive, avoided anything negative and continued to do business. I honestly learned to just keep going, especially when everyone else was in the coffee room complaining. Stay far away from negative people!

The market is the market, and I will always be ready for it. I keep going, so when it does change I am ready to go. There is a light at the end of the tunnel.

Every morning, I did research of new listings and then went on tour, usually with a group, from 10:00 a.m. until noon. In the afternoon, I would always call a minimum of five people (the more the better) from my personal contact list to just say hi and see how they were doing. I like a challenge, so I always tried to beat the number of contacts I made from the day before.

Depending on who I was calling and my relationship with that person, I might or might not talk about referrals. Was this the right time? I don't believe in pushing, and there is usually a right and wrong time for this part of the business, but again, this is only my personal view. We all have to figure out those times for ourselves.

People do forget that you are in real estate, so remind them, but be diplomatic. You do not want them to think that you are only calling them for referrals. You want to see how they are, re-establish contact if that is the case, and if real estate falls into the conversation, all the better.

Somehow, real estate *always* came into the conversation for me. I made sure it did.

Often I would send these people a handwritten general note, enclosing two business cards. Today, you could follow up with an e-mail or a handwritten note, depending on who it was that you were in touch with.

So here I was for months, doing everything I should be doing. I was in contact with everyone and anyone I could possibly be. I was cold-calling, which really wasn't my bag, but for me it beat door-knocking,

I knew the market inside and out, but where were the sellers and buyers? I couldn't find any.

It is very easy in this business to get down, depressed and discouraged, but you have to keep your ambition, drive and faith. Give yourself a kick in the butt if you start losing your self-confidence and feeling frustrated.

I was doing that too, but again, where were all the sellers and buyers?

Each day when you go to work, you just never know what is going to happen. It is definitely a constantly changing profession. I love that part of the business.

Do not get discouraged; it will happen.

CHAPTER 4
PROMOTION, ADVERTISING AND MARKETING

Whether you are new agent or an experienced pro who wants to revitalize your marketing material, one of the first items to select are colours that you will use consistently on everything. This is an inexpensive but good way to make your material recognizable, and that is the objective. Whenever someone sees certain colours—with or without a logo or mission statement—they will know it is from you. You must be consistent.

There are numerous ways you can advertise or promote yourself, and I'll review a few of them here.

Mission Statement

My personal mission statement is "Stay out of real estate jail," and it truly represents what I am all about. I care about the public and my colleagues, and I am constantly striving to find ways to help everyone. I will do anything I can to help keep agents from making any mistakes, especially those errors that could lead to discipline from our authorities. If I can make your real estate career easier, then I will try to assist you with whatever I have seen or been told or what has been recommended to me.

Suggestion: Think about what you would like to say about yourself and your beliefs and what you will do or are doing for your clients, customers and/or colleagues. Take the time to decide if you do want a personal mission statement, and then if so, think about the wording and what you want to convey to the public—why you are in the industry, what you will do for your clients and what special qualities you have.

Photographs

Once you have your colours set, the next question is, do you have a photograph of yourself? Decide whether you want your photo to be on your business cards, promotional sites and materials, including feature sheets for handing out when you are showing properties you have for sale.

Suggestion: Take a serious look at the photo you plan to use for your marketing. Is it you? Is it really you, and does it make a great first impression? If not, get a new one taken by a professional. Even if you are a seasoned professional, take another look at your photo—is it you?

Some licensees may prefer not to have a photo, and it is an item you should seriously think about. One of the pros is that when you hand out any materials people can put a face to your name, and in our industry you want everyone to know who you are and recognize you. The biggest con is that it could be a safety issue.

I once did have a chap follow me around like a lost puppy, drop in for coffee and even want me to teach him how to drive. My photo was everywhere so he knew exactly what I looked like. He became a bit infatuated, but it did not turn into anything problematic.

My photo was on my business cards, bus benches, my letterhead, faxes, etc. One day when he dropped into the office for coffee, I told him I was busy but my (male) partner would take him out to see properties from then on. That was the last time I ever saw him. Don't let this scare you, but you do have to think safety.

Business Cards

Always enclose two business cards with everything. Even if you are just paying a bill by mail or renewing a subscription, enclose two business cards. Okay, not with e-mails or faxes.

I used to think printing companies suggested this so you had to keep reordering more cards, but no, the main idea is that the receiver will keep one and give one to a friend, colleague or acquaintance. We know the odds are it will go in the trash, but it did work for me a number of times over the years, back when we had to pay bills by mail. Now I am really dating myself.

True Story

One day the phone rang and it was a young woman from B. C. Telephone. She said she was so tired of receiving all my business cards, but she wanted to buy and since she didn't know any other agents and she had hundreds of my cards in her drawer, she decided to call me. I actually found her a condominium to buy and a few years later sold that for her and bought her a new little house. We became friends, and I have worked with her and her acquaintances and friends ever since. So now I believe in the "two business card" rule.

Try to make it a habit that you always give out or enclose two business cards to everyone unless you know it is an inappropriate circumstance. I still do this today.

Suggestion: When you are in a restaurant and you have the most fantastic meal, awesome service and just the perfect night out, leave two business cards with the large tip. Let them know who you are and what you do. Now, if the service was awful, the food was blah, and you didn't leave a tip or you left a very small tip, *leave someone else's business card!* I am only kidding.

Other Marketing Materials

As real estate agents, we all know that marketing and promotional materials are important to help build our image and promote our services. The simplest form of marketing obviously is your business card with a photo that really is you, and we have now agreed to always give two business cards to everyone. You have chosen the colours you want to market with.

Think about this, though: every time you send an e-mail or fax, pay a bill, renew a subscription (yes, some still do this by mail), post a letter, or use a piece of paper, note, file folder, pen, envelope—these too could all be classed as promotional materials. Do they represent you? Can you be easily found?

You want to think about these items and include your name, your full brokerage name, your address, your phone number (always including your area code if applicable), your e-mail and your website.

Every time you e-mail, is the message you are sending promoting you? Is your mission statement and/or logo included on it? You definitely want your contact numbers. You want to be found. You never want to be missing in action.

What is written on the notes or messages you leave for people or send to others? Market and promote yourself to the fullest extent. It doesn't cost you any more money, so this is an easy way to start off or update as the case may be.

Are these items promoting you every time they are sent out? Remember, each and every piece of paper that you distribute is a marketing item for you, so when you get someone's attention, you want to make sure everything reflects well on you.

Design your own personalized notes for all general note cards and thank-you notes, letterhead, feature sheets, envelopes, faxes and everything you can think of. With today's technology, it will be easy for you to do or have a printer make a supply up for you with your return address and contact information on the envelopes in your colours, and maybe with your mission statement, logo and/or photo. Also put your phone numbers and e-mail address.

You could do this as well for the double-copy carbonless paper you will give to each of

17

your clients so you can keep a copy of the second page of what their comments were when viewing properties. (Look for "Form | Showings | Buyers Comments" on the website.) You want their feedback, comments and suggestions, so tearing off the second page is the perfect solution.

One form in particular you might want to be double-copy carbonless is the one on the website at "Buyers | Must Haves and Would Like." This is the form that they fill in to let you know what they are specifically looking for in their dream home, so it will help you narrow the search parameters. Test-drive these forms and see what the buyers actually fill in and don't fill in, and then you can redesign them or alter them and *only then* spend money to make them double-copy carbonless.

These notes and papers could be predesigned with your photo, brokerage logo and all your contact info. Don't forget to select a colour or two that will be on all your marketing materials. Just be careful that if your e-mail or other contact information is on a colour, it's easy to read.

When I am teaching and get the students' business cards, some of their e-mail or phone numbers are extremely difficult to read. This is because their phone number or e-mail is on a colour that blocks the reading of it, or they have it located where there is a design on the card that makes it hard to read. Be careful and consider this when choosing your colours and design materials.

Think big and make sure your impression/logo is very unique, professional and something the public will always relate to you the minute they see it. Don't forget to include any required disclaimers. See the form "Disclaimers | Samples" in the appendix and also on the website

This is not a "just do it" situation. Think about it and design something very special, distinguished and classic. Be professional. Depending on your mission statement, you could include that on everything as well.

You can also redesign sample faxes to include your photo, brokerage logo, etc., and double-check if you want to include the disclaimers at the bottom of the page. This can also be done on the return fax cover sheet addressed to you. However, on the return fax addressed to you, I do not include the disclaimer about breaching agency and I did not include using a return cover sheet. See the website for more information.

Newspaper and Magazine Advertising

Some local newspapers offer free advertising so you can announce you have proudly joined our industry and with which brokerage. If you live out of the area where this free service is offered, what's stopping you from letting people in that area know where you are and what you do? Think about newspapers around the world. Could this lead to referrals?

This free marketing can also be used if you have changed brokerages, done special community work, or reached specific goals or achievements. Just use it and research all newspapers in any areas where you know people—or maybe even where you don't know people—and submit your blurb with your photo.

Think outside the box: What could help you get some publicity and fantastic exposure, including referrals? Some agents even pay to have their photo and blurb in specific newspapers or magazines. The idea is to get your name and profession well-known. Don't be a secret agent.

Suggestion: When you send the information to newspapers or magazines, especially those that are free, you must ask them to please only run your blurb when it can be with your photo. People look at photographs first.

Real Estate Associations

Are you a member of other real estate associations throughout the world? Why not? Hello, referrals! Dream big but join now. International memberships are not that expensive. Don't just think Canada and the USA—what about Australia, England and all the other countries in the world?

Research and see just where you can position yourself and your marketing expertise and location, and as I said, think big. Don't limit yourself to just joining local associations or memberships. What about referral companies and the like? Can you arrange to be part of their networks?

Cold-Calling and Door-Knocking

Not very many agents are doing this today, especially with the "do not call" lists being enforced. I hated it personally, but that's what we did back then.

These particular items are more related to working with sellers, so I will not elaborate on them in this book. I will tell you that when I first started out, I did cold-call, because I didn't know what else to do at that time.

True Story

There was a colleague in my office who cold-called every single morning and door-knocked every afternoon, so I tried going door-knocking with him. I hated it. Cold-calling I did every day as well, and I was so used to hearing no that when someone said yes, they would like an evaluation, I said, "Thank you for your time and have a good day." When I hung up, I realized they said yes, so I called them right back, and they really did say yes. We laughed about it as I explained, and do you know what? In the end, I got the listing, and we became good friends. I don't think I will ever forget it.

Floor Duty

Many brokerages still offer floor-duty time. This is where, if a member of the public phoned or walked in and wanted some information on real estate, it would go to whoever was on floor duty.

True Story

The second week of my being a proud real estate agent who knew nothing, a chap came into our office and wanted to talk to a representative. Two ladies who worked together were on floor duty, so this was their lead. They peered around the corner and saw a fellow with torn jeans who looked pretty shabby. They didn't want to waste their time with him, so they asked me to go meet him.

I was new and still struggling, so for sure I would talk to him. Thanks, ladies! I grabbed my two business cards, my pen, and my Buyer's Information Record Sheet and introduced myself to him. He was the nicest man, and he had a wife and kids. I asked him all the questions from my Buyer's Information form, which I had in front of me, and we did a real—and I mean a *real*—interview. I actually prequalified him.

I was on top of the world, and I liked him. I wanted to work with him. To make a very long story short, it turned out this young man was a millionaire builder/developer. Well, so much for the shabby appearance! We started working together that very day, and over the years I sold him seven or eight properties. Thank goodness he wore torn jeans that day! That's all I can say.

P.S. When I met this chap, I didn't actually have a Buyer's Information form prepared, but I put it in so you would know what to use. I just once again played it by ear, but I did ask the right questions, and I did set him up with my mortgage broker, who I used for every client I ever met.

I still use the same mortgage broker today, and he has never let me down. He has even saved jeopardized closings in our brokerage in a day or two. You need to establish rapport with financial people and maybe even refer clients to each other.

I seemed to meet a number of people who didn't really want to tell me their financial situations. I always just referred everyone to my mortgage broker, who would then phone and tell me what price range they could afford and any other pertinent information I might need. It was fabulous, and my clients liked this way of doing business with me.

Suggestion: Whenever you first meet buyers, always arrange for them to get prequalified for financing. There is no sense working with them if you don't know how much they can afford and what their limits are. I have learned that the hard way.

Name Badge and REALTOR® Pin

I remember asking a group of students, "Who can you tell is a real estate agent?" Look around if you are at your office or outside or in the mall, the bank or anywhere. Are you a secret agent? Most people are. Why?

You don't need to wear a sidewalk sign stating your name and what you do; that just might be a bit excessive! But I do not understand why you aren't wearing your REALTOR® pin with pride, or even your office name badge.

Why are you a secret agent? Our business is a people business, and everyone loves talking about real estate. No matter what they have to say, the public loves to talk real estate. I have built some fabulous relationships with people in the line-up at the bank, the grocery store and the malls—in fact, everywhere. I am not a secret agent.

Wear your name badge or your REALTOR® pin with pride and dignity. I try to have my REALTOR® pin or name badge on all my jackets, but I will warn you now, if you are partying, having a few cold ones, or getting road rage, for goodness sakes *remove* your identification. That would *not* be a good thing. We don't want the public to know who we are if we are not in our top professional form.

True Story

Here's one of those times when you *should* be a secret agent. My father, Lyall O. Bell, Vice-President of Sauder Industries and also the Commodore of the Royal Vancouver Yacht Club, was down at the Seattle Yacht Club for opening day. We were on his boat, the *Four Bells*. Bob Hope was on his ocean liner down the dock, so my dad decided he was going to meet the actor no matter what.

Dad waited and waited, all the while having a few very large martinis, when finally Bob Hope came down the ramp toward his boat. This was after a few hours of waiting, but my dad jumped up, went out on the dock and said, "Mr. Hope, I am Lyall O. Bell, and I am a

Canadian." At that point, my dad—obviously after a few too many—tripped walking toward Bob Hope and fell flat on his face.

I don't think I have ever laughed so hard in my life. Mr. Hope stopped, turned and walked over to Dad. Looking down at him sprawled on the wharf, he said, "By God, you *are* a Canadian."

Here's another true story from my experience. I was teaching about seventy agents one day, and there was one very experienced seasoned REALTOR® in the room. I mentioned wearing your REALTOR® pin. She groaned very loudly and said something like, "You have to be kidding us." I wasn't kidding anyone. Do you want to be a secret agent? Don't you want people to know what you do?

I am so proud of my profession that I tell everyone who will listen to me. In my mind, I thought, *Why are you pretending to be a real estate agent when it is so obvious you hate your job and to you it is nothing but work?* To me, real estate is never work. Maybe she was a sister of Negative Nellie. It may be time for her to leave our industry, because if you aren't truly ecstatic and passionate about who and what you are and what you are doing, and if you don't wake up thinking *I wonder what's in store for me today*, it might be time to move on.

I always wonder what positive wonderful thing is in store for me today. Who knows when that phone will ring? I am fiercely proud to be a real estate agent, and I absolutely love our industry.

Suggestion: I am not a secret agent because I wear my name badge or REALTOR® pin with incredible pride and confidence. I wear it almost everywhere so people know I am a professional real estate agent, and let's face it—most people want to talk about real estate. It is a fantastic way to meet new clients. I would never be a secret agent unless the circumstances called for it. I am certain you could recognize those types of situations when it would be inappropriate.

Signage

What about your open-house arrows and car-top signs—is your name and cell number (including area code if applicable) printed on these? I have personally driven by a business and wished I could call from the car if they were just closing or if I was on my way to an appointment and didn't have time to stop and run in.

Make it easy to find you. The other bonus is that the neighbours see your signs and arrows and know you are out working in their area *again.* They notice how often you are around, and that could lead to more business. It is obvious that you work hard, so you must be an expert in the neighbourhood.

Contracts of Purchase and Sale

When you are preparing an offer on your authorities' contracts, you will see where you disclose your agency representation a spot for your name as the representing agent. In our contracts, this is on the page where both the sellers and buyers sign. I call it the action page. Are you adding in your cell-phone number and e-mail address?

Make it easy for the listing agents to find you if they have a quick question. No one wants to search through a briefcase, wallet or purse to track down your cell number or to quickly text or e-mail you. Not only that, if you were in a multiple-offer situation and the sellers had a concern, you could actually win the bidding war if they can find you quickly.

Numerous agents were thrilled to learn this tip; it has worked, and their buyers did win the contract.

These are just a few simple ideas, but you should start implementing them today. If you don't have extra money for marketing materials, don't worry about it, you can redesign and pay for the upgrades as you do more business.

For now, though, at least have the photo. Start thinking about your mission statement if you want to use one. Think about the colours. You can implement the items costing money later, but for now, start using the ideas.

Don't procrastinate by saying, "I don't have this ready to go, so I will wait until I do!" That isn't going to cut it. Just use whatever you have for now. The designing and preparation can be done as a filler project during your low-time hours or days.

Chapter 5
Know the Market

It is your responsibility to make sure you know the market thoroughly. You have that duty and obligation to your clients and customers.

True Story

I found it educational and enjoyable going on tour with a group. We often discussed how they came up with that price, or we did sometimes say, "Wow, they bought that listing," since it was so overpriced. One day I jokingly asked a group of colleagues, as we stood in the seller's kitchen, "Don't the owners know that yellow walls with bright green and orange flooring is ugly?"

All of a sudden I heard this throat clearing sound *"ahem"* very loudly and realized one of the owners was sitting in the den right beside the kitchen. I was very lucky that he didn't know which one of us was so rude and had degraded his home, but I did learn a very big lesson: Watch what you say. I never said another word while we finished touring the house; I didn't want him to recognize my voice.

Suggestion: Go on tour every day if you possibly can. Diarize the times as appointments with yourself. Review the MLS® Hot Sheets daily and keep an eye on what is happening in the marketplace. Always be educated and knowledgeable.

Collaborating with Colleagues

You must know the market—what is for sale or sold, what has expired (possibly due to overpricing), how long specific properties are sitting on the market prior to selling, the number of price reductions and any other available information. You must know the market in order to help the public and in order to be professional.

As I mentioned earlier, I loved going on tour with my colleagues. Since we often carpooled, I would get to hear their thoughts on the pricing and other properties that were coming onto the market, and from that I developed a good sense of the "pulse" of the market. It was the best way for me to be educated and to work with my colleagues and my clients. (Now you have to be careful about these types of discussions.)

We shared information and co-operated with each other. If they had a new listing coming up, they often would let me know if it would suit any of the buyers I was working with, and I reciprocated. It was a win-win situation for all of us.

This type of co-operation made us all more money by sharing information and working together. It was great. Today, though, you really need your seller's permission regarding what you can and cannot share with others.

When your buyers are ready to make an offer, you will want to prepare an up-to-date Comparable Market Analysis (CMA) so they can make an informed decision about the price they are going to offer. You will provide them with all the facts, data and other research you can, including other properties for sale, recent sold prices, price changes and houses that are off the market or expired. You want to make sure their final decision of what to offer is based on true market conditions and accurate information.

CHAPTER 6
A REAL ESTATE AGENT'S JOB DESCRIPTION

What do you think is the most important and critical part of being a real estate agent? I believe it is that you must know how to write an enforceable Contract of Purchase and Sale, but not waste too much time doing it. Be prepared so you can be out there creating more business for yourself.

If you have it all organized and your checklists are in place, you could double or triple your income by getting more and more business, and you will be able to handle it. You can take your business as far as you want. No problem.

You need to make your first priority generating more business by prospecting—meeting with more and more sellers and buyers. If your contract writing is in order, then that's it, it's done, and you can get out there and create the business. You must absolutely focus on meeting people and creating business, and that will in turn automatically increase your bank account.

Seriously, you cannot prospect if you are worried about what to do when they are ready to make an offer. If you follow these guidelines, you are ready when they are, and you won't have to worry about anything. You have preplanned for the contract, leaving you lots and lots of time to get the business. *So go get it!*

Remember, real estate must be in writing, so it is imperative you know what you are doing in order to protect everyone who is party to the transaction, and that includes you. Poorly written offers, lazy offers, shortcut offers or sloppy offers reflect badly on the agents and to the public, and they are certainly of no benefit to help your buyers purchase a property.

It is not the job of the listing agents to rewrite your statements and subjects just because you didn't do it correctly. We are professionals. Please be skilful and do it right the first time. There is no such thing as a do-over. Take your time.

True Story

I remember a few broker/owners telling me that their sales force didn't need to worry about writing a contract. They felt that their agents needed to get out there and get business. They could worry about the "contract bit" when they found someone who wanted to sell or buy.

I will never forget the first seller and buyer I dealt with. I lost both those transactions by not knowing how to write a proper contract or what to do. I sincerely believe that if you are truly professional and have your systems in place for writing a contract, you can relax knowing that if a buyer wants to buy or a seller wants to sell, you will know exactly what to do.

Organizing Your Contract

Ask yourself: How long would it take you to have a Contract of Purchase and Sale ready for the parties to sign?

If you are organized, you may be one of the lucky few agents that I surveyed who said fifteen minutes, because they had all the templates done for their clauses and phrases. Or you may take an average of an hour to an hour and a half. Some agents can take four or five hours to get everything organized and ready to go, but this does not include checking for omitted statements/subjects or errors.

The length of time really depends a lot on the complexity of the offer, but if you are spending hours and hours writing an offer, you could be doing something wrong. Maybe your statements start out okay, then all of a sudden a couple of subjects appear and then some more statements, so you see what I am getting at. There is absolutely no semblance of order, and that makes it twice as hard and time-consuming.

It is here that you are prone to forgetting something. Add to that the pressure of having clients sitting across from you, and it can make for a very dangerous contract process. So take it step by step and in the same order every time to get rid of this type of problem.

Set up your contracts so you don't forget anything. You have your checklists and your statements all in one place and ready to cut, copy and paste into your particular contract. Your subjects are also ready to go, and you just need to choose the ones applicable to the property.

Remember, there really are only three main financing subjects, so pick one. Depending on the market in your area, you may also have to select the financing clause that allows the sellers to make certain they have enough money to pay everyone off and to pay you.

You could be in a market where the buyers are asking the sellers to carry the mortgage, which means you would vary from the usual three financing clauses—but other than that, it is really very straightforward. So let's get to the nuts and bolts of writing an enforceable Contract of Purchase and Sale.

Suggestion: Stop procrastinating and take the time to set everything in motion to fulfill your dreams and become a fiercely proud real estate agent. I know that by following these steps, new agents will reduce the anxiety that comes with being asked to write an offer and seasoned agents will avoid the mistakes that often come with complacency. When everything is in place and once you use the system a few times, you will have more time and energy to devote to your clients.

CHAPTER 7
COMMON CONTRACT STATEMENTS

When you are writing any Contract of Purchase and Sale, you want to review 32 statements that could or should be in most of your contracts. I will start with an indexed list of each of the 32 possible statements and then provide the wording you could use for each. In that wording:

- *Italics*, [brackets] or <u>underlined</u> portions of the statement indicate that you need to take some form of action prior to using the clause. You may need to add your authorities' regulations or the name of your professional act, or simply revise the statement to suit your needs.

- [   ] indicates you must fill in information or delete it.

- [_____] indicates you must fill in information or delete it.

Each statement appears in its own section along with any explanations for using the statement, any information that may help clarify why you may want to include the statement, and a few sample discipline cases if they are applicable to the topic. Occasionally, you will find suggestions relating to the statement.

Always start your contract addendums with statements and, in particular, with confirmations that your clients were afforded the opportunity to seek independent legal professional advice. This is absolutely crucial and must be in all your Contracts of Purchase and Sale. The onus of proof is on you.

The items follow a specific order, so you must be methodical and keep them in the same format for every contract. This will help chart your course by being consistent so you will not forget anything. You can use the detailed information to clarify any concerns with your clients if needed.

You want to very simply demonstrate and illustrate why they will be protected by having particular statements in the contract. It is your job to counsel and advise your clients why these are important protections and also if the statements are necessary or not depending on the specific type of property they are buying.

You must possess impeccable skills and establish, if you are new representative, or re-establish, if you are a seasoned pro, the best comprehensive Contract of Purchase and Sale that will always safely protect your clients. If you employ the methods provided here, you will provide top-notch service to everyone.

The word will soon spread throughout our industry and to real estate buyers and sellers who will begin seeking you out for your assistance and guidance. They will want to work with an agent like you who is known to be trustworthy, determined, precise and cautious, and who genuinely represents the client's interests.

Now, let's look at the headings of the possible statements you could use in most of your Contracts of Purchase and Sale.

1. Legal/Professional Advice | Standard Care

2. Acceptance of All Statements

3. Access for All Trades

4. Appliances—Buyers' Acceptance Of

5. Furniture or Other Items/Equipment Being Sold by Sellers

6. Rental or Leased Agreements/Contracts

7. Confidentiality Agreement

8. Deposits | Legal Advice

9. Deposits—If Any Interest Is Accrued

10. Incorporation of Documents

11. Measurements/Room Sizes/Square Footage/Lot Size/Age

12. No Growth or Manufacture of Illegal Substances

13. Outstanding Orders

14. Plans/Permits/Documents/Drawings Will Be Supplied by the Sellers

15. Property Disclosure

16. Referral Fee Disclosure

17. Remuneration Disclosure

18. Registering in Another Name [Do Not Use and/or Nominee]

19. Residents

20. Returning of the Sellers' Documents

21. Sellers Agree to Allow Time for Buyers to Remove Subjects

22. Sellers Have Disclosed Material Latent Defects

23. Sellers Hereby Authorize Buyers to Obtain Documents and Information [This Puts the Buyers in the Sellers' Shoes]

24. Sellers Will Sign Necessary Documentation and Allow Access

25. Separate Disclosures | Statements

26. Survey

27. Taxes | Accounting/Professional Advice

28. Taxes | Property Assessments

29. Taxes | Property Transfer Tax Statement

30. Title Insurance

31. Title Search

32. Waiver of Subjects

1. Legal/Professional Advice | Standard Care

The [Sellers/Buyers or the Sellers and Buyers] acknowledge that the Agents/Representatives/ Brokerages providing agency services to the Sellers and Buyers do not provide Legal/Professional/ Accounting/Construction/Engineering/Environmental/Tax/Zoning or other expert advice in matters beyond the common standard of care in the Real Estate Industry. The parties have been [afforded the opportunity and] advised to seek independent or other expert advice [and waived their right to do so] prior to entering into this Contract of Purchase and Sale [and warrant and guarantee that they shall hold harmless and indemnify the Sellers' and Buyers' Agents/Representatives/ Brokerages from any claims, actions or causes of action that may be the result of any and all issues or uses of the land/property/buildings/structures].

Explanation

You have a duty to make this a subject if you are concerned about anything. This statement appears in numerous contracts. I personally believe that it should be in every Contract of Purchase and Sale that you write.

If you are writing an offer on Friday night at 7:00 p.m. and put this statement in the contract, the buyers may ask you how they can get legal/professional or other advice on a Friday night. Your answer is truthful and very simple: You have reviewed the contract, the statements, the subjects, the property specifics and the preprinted wording with them, and if they have any concerns or questions, then you will make it a subject. Most will be just fine with that, and if they are not, then obviously you do make it a subject. This explanation could also apply to sellers.

I personally am not sure if your clients will accept the end of this statement, where it states that they will hold the agents/representatives/brokerages harmless. However, this has been included in a few contracts.

When offering legal and professional advice as a subject, I do understand your concerns. I once had a lawyer tell my clients that they should have had her write the contract, not me. That has happened more than once, and I know it is still happening. You could counteract this by being very specific as to what you want the lawyer to review—for example, the actual charges on the Title Search only.

Sample Discipline Cases

Important: Here and in the Sample Discipline Cases throughout the book, I have just paraphrased case samples, and they may be missing other mistakes the agents made. It is only to give you an idea of what can happen. Also, if the agents preagreed to a "consent order" with their authorities, the penalties were often much lower than they would initially have been.

Legal/Professional Advice

An agent and/or brokerage failed to:

- advise the buyers to seek independent legal advice with respect to the Contract of Purchase and Sale. (You have no idea how many of these disciplinary reprimands were in the case samples. It would boggle your mind.)

- ensure that the seller sought independent representation or legal advice when he had his clients sign a fee agreement that purported to change the agency relationship from a limited dual agency relationship to no agency.

- advise the clients to seek independent legal advice prior to entering into the contract.

- advise the clients to seek independent advice and/or independent legal advice with respect to the value of the property and/or the terms and conditions of the contract.

- document his advice and the fact that the parties were advised to seek independent legal advice as to financing, mortgage and development issues.

- recommend to the seller that the seller should obtain either independent legal advice or independent appraisal advice or both before accepting the offer.

Reasonable Skill and Care

An agent and/or brokerage failed to:

- show the "actual" subject removal date and backdated it a week or so earlier.

- disclose information and/or provide copies of all relevant documents to the buyer so that the buyer would be aware of all material information regarding the property.

- use reasonable efforts to discover relevant facts respecting the property.

- draft the contract with reasonable care and skill.

- ensure the contract fully clarified all terms and conditions.

- act with reasonable care and skill when drafting a Contract of Purchase and Sale without a completion date.

- use clear terms with respect to an agreement for sale; the vagueness of the terms used could render the contract unenforceable.

- act with reasonable care and skill by failing to keep their clients apprised of price changes on the MLS® listing for the property.

- use reasonable care and skill, in that the second sale contract was dated December 1 when in fact the second sale contract was entered into on December 16.

- take reasonable steps to avoid a conflict of interest, in that he acted for the buyers and at the same time prepared and presented an offer to purchase the property by his bride-to-be, and failed to promptly and fully disclose the conflict of interest in that he did not inform the buyers of his fiancé's interest in the property or of the fact that he planned to prepare and present an offer by his bride-to-be to purchase the property.

- act honestly and/or use reasonable care and skill.

- act in the best interests of the seller, thereby putting the seller in potential financial jeopardy by leading the seller to believe that the listing contract was cancelled on payment of the remuneration and that the seller was no longer obliged to pay a commission to the brokerage upon the sale of the property when the listing contract was still in force and the seller's obligations were intact.

- ensure that the contract set out the completion date intended by the seller.

- use reasonable care and skill in that he did not verify the lot size of the property on behalf of his clients before they entered into a Contract of Purchase and Sale.

- use reasonable efforts to discover relevant facts and failed to act with reasonable care and skill, in that he failed to make inquiries as to whether the wall had been constructed inside the setback.

- show competence regarding the marketing and sale of lots.

- draft the Contracts of Purchase and Sale with reasonable care and skill.

- ensure that the sellers had all of the information upon which they could make an informed decision as to how to proceed.

- use reasonable care and skill in that the Contract of Purchase and Sale did not contain the full details of the agreement between the parties.

Another agent favoured his own buyer's offer over others, thereby failing to act in the seller's best interest when he permitted one buyer's offer to be dealt with by the seller prior to the expiry of the time he had set for dealing with the offers, and another agent allowed a client to use the brokerage computer.

Comments

Do you see how unnecessary all these discipline cases really were? There is absolutely no reason a licensee should have to face a discipline hearing for these types of concerns.

You have to take your time, and you must always offer independent legal/professional advice to your clients and confirm this in writing in your contract. If there is any concern or hesitation by the clients, you must make it a subject to obtaining independent legal/ professional advice.

I have included this clause to be in statements that could be in your contracts so you will never forget it. Again though, if there are any worries, you make it a subject and that's that.

2. Acceptance of All Statements

*The [Sellers/Buyers or the Sellers and Buyers] have been advised prior to entering into this Contract of Purchase and Sale that if any of the Statements/wording in this Contract of Purchase and Sale are a concern or they want further explanation/clarification they must make them a subject to their investigation/research and not remain as accepted and acknowledged statements. The [Sellers/Buyers or the Sellers and Buyers] confirm they are in agreement with any and all Statements/wording as written and are aware of any possible ramification of this legal, binding and enforceable Contract of Purchase and Sale.

Explanation

This is self-explanatory.

3. Access for All Trades

*The Sellers, at no cost to the Sellers, [unless otherwise mutually agreed to in writing] warrant and guarantee to allow access to the land/property/buildings/structures by any of the trades for their purpose on reasonable [or 24 hours] [written] notice, including but not limited to Appraisers, Engineers, Environmentalists, Financiers, Inspectors, Insurers, Surveyors or other Professional Agents/Representatives of the Buyers' choice.
OR
The Sellers consent and will allow access to the property by any of the 'trades' for their purpose on reasonable notice, including but not limited to financiers, appraisers, insurers, surveyors and inspectors.*[You may want to insert a time frame they are allowed in.]
It is mutually agreed and confirmed that the Buyers/Buyers' Agents or Representatives may accompany the trades when they access.
You may want to insert a time frame | e.g. within [____calendar] days of acceptance of this Contract of Purchase and Sale by all parties or [an actual date – e.g. 3 days before the subject removal date – e.g. 3 days before all subject removals is September 15th therefore use September 12th as the date] and in some cases it may even be [completion date].

Explanation

You have a duty to protect the public by using reasonable care and skill. What has happened in the past is that sometimes buyers choose not to include some or all of the subjects, and the agents forget to include allowing for access if required.

This has happened numerous times where the buyers did not include a "subject to financing," and yet the financial institution wanted an appraisal no matter how small the amount of financing the buyers required. This seems to be standard procedure with banks and mortgage brokers.

True Story

An appraiser called to do an inspection and the sellers said no, you cannot come onto our property; the buyers had a subject-free offer. This generated numerous visits with the lawyers on a purchase that hadn't even completed, but it was a firm no-subject contract.

This has also reared itself relating to insurance on some specific types of properties. Again, the sellers refused to allow the insurance people onto the property because there were no subjects and therefore no statement allowing the insurance representatives, like the bank affiliates, to enter the property for purposes of insurance.

This has been a major concern in our industry recently and has caused nothing but serious problems. It is your responsibility to protect your buyers, and since you know that the financial people will almost always want to do an appraisal even for a small loan amount or a line of credit, you must protect your buyers by making sure that access for all trades is provided.

If you remember to put this access in with your statements that could be in most contracts, it guarantees that you will not forget to do your due diligence representing your buyers. There is no reason whatsoever for not representing them to the highest standards, and that means allowing access for trades that may be required.

This same scenario has happened with regards to oil/septic tanks and the like. The buyers do not want a "subject to" clause, but they may want or need to send a trade in to verify any worries or concerns they have.

The above statement allows access for appraisers, engineers, environmentalists, financiers, inspectors, insurers, surveyors or other professional agents/representatives of the buyer's choice to be able to access the property and structures if required. It also confirms that this is at no cost to the sellers; however, you could negotiate in your contract exactly who will pay for any costs.

It is your responsibility to see that this is covered in writing in the contract. Put this in every contract you write, and you will always be able to get the mortgage people or insurance people or others on the property should the need arise. You will not forget.

Our level of expertise and knowledge requires that we use common sense, standards of care and professionalism. Since this has now become a common occurrence in our industry, it is your responsibility to protect your buyers.

Allowing access for any of these professionals does not necessarily mean that the buyers can escape the contract. The sellers often say no because:

1. It was not specifically requested in the contract.

2. The sellers are worried that the buyers may want out of the purchase if they find something wrong or if the property was under-appraised or was not insurable, as per the above example.

In a nutshell, make access for all trades a standard statement in all of your contracts.

4. Appliances—Buyers' Acceptance of

*The Buyers understand and acknowledge that the Sellers are not making any express or implied warranties/guarantees and that while the included items will be in substantially the same condition on possession date as when viewed, they are not new and as such are not guaranteed or warranted by the Sellers. The Sellers, at no cost to the Sellers, agree to provide appliance manuals, instruction manuals and warranty information applicable to any appliances/chattels/equipment/fixtures included in the purchase price, if available on or before possession date.
OR
*Within *[3 calendar]* days of acceptance of this Contract of Purchase and Sale by all Parties, the Sellers will provide a signed and dated list of the make/brand name, model, serial number and colour of all appliances included at no cost to the Buyers or the Buyers' Agents/Representatives/Brokerage; which will be incorporated into and form part of this contract. The Sellers, at no cost to the Sellers, agree to provide appliance manuals, instruction manuals and warranty information applicable to any appliances/chattels/equipment/fixtures included in the purchase price, if available.

Explanation

We sell dirt.

Sometimes I think I should have opened my own appliance store: *Barb's Microwaves ... but wait ... if you buy today ... save ...*

You would not believe the number of microwaves I had to purchase over my career because I asked for the appliances in good working order. We do not sell appliances, remove rubbish or professionally clean carpets.

We sell dirt. End of story.

Do not request these items unless you are willing to pay for them in the future. We do not sell appliances, and we cannot and should not guarantee they will be in working order.

I also should have opened my own garbage removal company: *Barb's Rubbish Removal ... but wait ... today only ... two loads for the price of one ...*

I should have bought a truck to remove rubbish and garbage. At least I could have advertised my name and brokerage on the truck panels.

We do not professionally clean carpets. What exactly does that mean?

Does it mean the sellers have to hire a company to steam-clean the carpets and in which rooms, or can the sellers just rent a machine?

I have never seen so many agents paying for these items out of their hard-earned commissions. I don't believe that you should ever cut your commission unless it is absolutely the end of the line, so why would you spend your money on an appliance, removing garbage or cleaning?

True Story

A colleague had already learned from previous mistakes to make sure she used the above statement regarding the appliances, cleaning carpets and removing rubbish. She was very clear about it; she had been caught up in these situations before, and of course when there is a problem, the listing agent does not know where to find the sellers. They are always missing in action.

This was different, though. This was her very best friend, so she decided to guarantee the appliances would all be in working order. I mean, come on, let's protect our best friends, our families and those close to us.

Well, move-in day comes and goes, and a week or so later the agent gets a call from her very best friend. The friend was so upset you wouldn't believe it. She told the agent that the fridge *hummed*. It *hummed*, and it was loud and bothersome. The agent called the listing agent, who had no idea where the sellers had moved to. Of course, they are always missing in action. Uh oh, here we go again!

In the end, the agent bought a new fridge for $1,200 for her very best friend. Why? Because she was trying to protect her. However, she did say I could tell the story, because she knew she should have used the above appliance statement.

She said she would never offer appliances in good working order again. How could she? She doesn't know if they will work two months later, or for that matter, how does she know they even work now? How could any of us agents know?

I don't know how solid their friendship is today. A *humming fridge* of all things!

P.S. My big thing was always microwaves. For some reason, the day after move-in they blew up. Figure that one out. It was incredible how many times I bought new microwaves before I learned my lesson. I must be a very slow learner.

We do not sell appliances, we do not clean carpets, and we certainly do not remove rubbish! We sell dirt. That's it! We sell dirt. I don't know how I can make this any clearer.

You work so very hard for your commission, so why on earth (dirt!) are you buying appliances? Why are you cleaning carpets? Why are you removing rubbish and garbage?

Come on, we sell dirt! Please don't blow your hard-earned money on the above three items. It's crazy.

A colleague made a sale on a new home to his buyers and stated in the contract that the walls would be finished in the same workmanlike manner as the rest of the building, the walls would be painted in eggshell white, the carpets would be professionally cleaned, and the grass would be cut on or before completion date.

On Saturday, just before completion date, I drove by the property, and there was my real estate agent painting the interior of the house. A professional cleaning truck was parked out front, and then on Sunday when I drove by again, my colleague was cutting the grass. He missed two full days of taking clients out looking at properties to buy or holding his own open house trying to attract some clients or just spending some time with his family and friends. I often wonder what those two days actually cost him personally.

I even know of agents who thought they were doing a favour for their family or friends and so did include the wording that all appliances will be in working order, all the rubbish will be removed and all the carpets will be professionally cleaned. They were just trying to help their family or friends, but it normally doesn't work out that way.

Seriously, why should you have to use part of your hard-earned commission to remove rubbish, repair or replace appliances, or professionally clean carpets? By the way, can you define what "professionally cleaned" means? I doubt it. It will never mean the same to two people. If you allow this type of wording in your contract, you might as well get out your wallet right now.

There is a war today about cleaning the carpets. The sellers rented a machine, but the buyers wanted a professional company. Now everyone is arguing. What are the odds that the agents end up paying a professional carpet-cleaning company?

Often what transpires is that there is a dispute over appliances working, garbage being left on the property and/or the carpets being cleaned. Once the buyers make their concern known, their agent contacts the listing agent who usually states that he or she doesn't know where the sellers are; they are missing in action. Now the agent for the buyers has a decision to make: to contribute to the cost to fix the problem to keep the rapport, or to walk away from giving any assistance. Quite often the agent succumbs to the buyers' demands just to make life easier. Please do not put yourself in this position.

If, though, there is an old beat-up car on the property, a pile of wood and bags of garbage, you want to make sure these are removed. You must be specific in identifying what the sellers must remove, including the location of the debris. Remember, when you are writing a contract, you are pretending it is you or your family buying the property—so you would ask yourself, what if the sellers do not remove the specifically identified debris? Maybe you consider a hold-back?

Suggestion: When you list the chattels and appliances included in the sale, always state "at no extra cost." At least you are being specific that the sellers are not charging for any of the items, and they are just included with the sale. This may one day be added protection if the government ever tries to charge for tax on the resale of the items.

5. Furniture or Other Items/Equipment Being Sold by Sellers

*The Sellers warrant and guarantee to give the Buyers the right of first refusal to negotiate for the purchase of any furniture or items/equipment to be sold by the Sellers upon a mutually agreed written price between the Sellers and Buyers. The parties are aware there may be a tax involved, applicable to the sale of such items and have been advised to confirm with their *[Accountant/ Income Tax Department/Legal or Professional Advisors or your Authorities/Regulators]* prior to entering into any separate written agreement. Should the Sellers and Buyers not come to a mutual agreement on or before *[date]* the Buyers' right of first refusal shall become null and void and the Sellers are able to negotiate or contract with others. This separate written purchase and sale for furniture or other items/equipment is for the benefit of the Sellers and Buyers and will be negotiated privately between the parties and not form part of this Contract of Purchase and Sale. Time shall remain of the essence.

Explanation

This is self-explanatory, but I will warn you that there are areas where the governments do charge tax on furniture that is sold, so be very careful. This has happened twice that I personally know of, but it is much easier to let the sellers and buyers work out their own sale for furniture or other similar items.

True Story

There was a very lucky young lady who won a lottery-prize home, but she could not afford the taxes so she listed the property for sale a year or two later. The brand-new furniture was included in the sale, and the government did step in and collect tax on the resale of these items. This is just like it is with vehicles—each time they are sold, the government gets its share. The buyers were upset because their agent did not warn them that this could possibly happen. They did settle privately, and I am sure from the rumour mill that it was an expensive settlement.

Think of the time the agent had to spend worrying about the case brought against him or her, and the energy wasted preparing statements for the defence of which there really wasn't any such thing.

The stress took a real toll on the licensee as well. The agent was held responsible for not giving the buyers professional advice that could affect their decision in buying the property.

6. Rental or Leased Agreements/Contracts

*It is a fundamental term of this Contract of Purchase and Sale that if any item/service *[e.g. alarm system, washer/dryer]* is under contract/monitor/lease/rental, the Sellers shall terminate and pay off such Contracts in full prior to completion at no cost to the Buyers.
[Do you want to ask the Sellers to leave the e. g. non-operating alarm system in place]?

Explanation

This is self-explanatory, but if you put it in your statements that could be in most of your contracts, you will not forget to review it and protect your buyers.

Often in a multi-unit complex, the (coin-operated) washer and dryer are leased, so please be careful. I did include a coin-operated washer and dryer once. I was able to settle with the buyers and it wasn't too expensive, but truthfully, why didn't I pay more attention when I was showing the property? I should have noticed they were coin-operated and then found out if they were leased. I was very lucky, since the lease was ending prior to completion date, but again, by being careless, I made a big mistake that could have been very expensive and stressful to fix.

7. Confidentiality Agreement

*The Sellers and Buyers have signed separately in writing and prior to entering into this Contract of Purchase and Sale a Confidentiality Agreement which is incorporated and forms part of this Contract of Purchase and Sale and all parties warrant and guarantee to abide by the Confidentiality Agreement unless otherwise mutually agreed to in writing by the Sellers and Buyers.

Explanation

Do you use a confidentiality statement in the contract, or do you use a confidentiality agreement entered into prior to entering into an agreement?

Some agents put a statement in the contract about confidentiality, but think about this: If you are in a multiple-offer situation—and that can be just two offers—and the sellers do not accept your offer, will the confidentiality statement apply? Remember, they didn't accept your offer.

The safest way to guarantee confidentiality is to predisclose it and have an agreement signed *prior* to presenting any offer. Put it on top of the contract and have everyone sign it before even looking at the offer. You would have a cross-referenced receipt of it (as per the above statement) in the contract as you do with any other separate disclosures. This is the safest course to protect all parties.

A confidentiality agreement can include various items that are to remain private, including the buyers' price and terms not being used to shop other offers, keeping financial statements and the like confidential, or rents not being disclosed. Using a confidentiality agreement really is the way to go.

8. Deposits | Legal Advice

> *The *[Sellers/Buyers or the Sellers and Buyers]* hereby acknowledge that they have been advised to obtain independent Legal/Professional advice before signing or accepting this Contract of Purchase and Sale with respect to the arrangements for holding the deposit monies in this transaction.

Explanation

You have a duty to make this a subject if your clients are concerned about anything, and you have a duty to protect the public by using reasonable care and skill. Remember, the deposit is the public's money. It is extremely critical that your clients understand where their money is going, who is looking after it and whether it is being held as a stakeholder. Is their money safe?

According to Barron's Law Dictionary, Sixth Edition, a stakeholder is "a third party chosen by two or more persons to keep in deposit … money the right or possession of which is contested between them."

The buyer's representative is not a stakeholder until there is an *accepted* offer. When brokerages are stakeholders, they cannot release a deposit to any of the buyers or any of the sellers without the written consent of every seller and every buyer in the sale, even if they wrote such instructions in the Contract of Purchase and Sale.

Sample Discipline Cases

An agent:

- was disciplined for numerous items, but one of them included that he forgot to put a clause in the Contract of Purchase and Sale recommending the buyers obtain independent legal advice with respect to the deposit arrangements. Penalty: suspended for approximately three weeks, a fine of $3,000 and completion of educational courses.

- entered into a consent order agreeing he had committed professional misconduct by not notifying the sellers immediately in writing that the deposit was not received as stated in the contract. Penalty: a fine of $750.

An agent and/or brokerage failed to:

- ensure that trust deposits were made payable "in trust."

- have the parties execute a separate agreement that the deposit would be paid directly to the seller by said buyers.

- have the parties sign an agreement that the deposit be paid to the seller's lawyer and did not advise the buyers to obtain independent legal advice with respect to the deposit arrangements.

- advise the buyers that they released a deposit to the sellers without a written agreement of the parties to the contract.

- obtain a written agreement separate from the Contract of Purchase and Sale when the deposit would not be held by the brokerage.

- write the deposit intentions in the contract that included paying non-refundable deposit instalments directly to the sellers.

- immediately notify the managing broker that the deposit was late and not in compliance with the contract.

- promptly deliver the deposit received from his buyer client to the brokerage.

- promptly deliver to his brokerage the remuneration received from the seller, for deposit into the trust account of the brokerage.

- ensure that deposit money was held in a trust account.

- account for and pay over, within a reasonable time, money that was received from buyers for deposits on a purchase.

- immediately notify his managing broker that the initial had not been received from the buyer within 48 hours of acceptance.

- ensure that, where the licensee held the funds and the deposit was to be paid directly to the sellers, there was an executed written agreement separate from any agreement giving effect to the trade in real estate.

- secure a separate written agreement that the deposit money would be paid to a party other than the trust account of the brokerage, in that the deposit was to be paid directly to the seller and the receipt indicated that this deposit was provided to the seller by the agent on behalf of the buyer.

- secure a separate written agreement that the deposit relating to the purchase and sale of the property would be held by someone other than his brokerage.

- deliver funds received from the buyer to the brokerage.

- advise the clients involved in those transactions to seek independent legal advice when the deposit was to be held by the seller's lawyers, someone other than the brokerage.

- ensure that the buyer was advised to seek independent legal advice with respect to paying the deposit directly to the seller.

- notify the managing broker that the deposit to be paid pursuant to the first sale contract was not paid.

- provide when the deposit was payable.

Comments

This is crazy! I only gave a few examples of the problems regarding deposits. You have to be very careful. The deposit money is the buyer's money! Don't ever forget that.

You can make it very easy for yourself by remembering to put the deposit in the buyer's brokerage (or escrow depending on your local market area) where it belongs. If it is going anywhere else, just know you are going to have to do a whole bunch of paperwork. Again, you must always offer independent legal/professional advice specifically relating to the deposits, including stating any ramifications of what can happen depending on where it is going. Always!

The easiest and smartest way is to put it in the buyer's brokerage/escrow where it belongs, *please.* None of these samples needed to have happened if someone had taken a little more time and thought it through.

I personally do not feel that these types of cases should ever go before a discipline hearing; there is absolutely no need for agents to be spending days preparing a feeble excuse for why they didn't follow the rules. Just obey the rules and regulations in your market area regarding where deposits belong and stick to it.

I also believe our authorities must be extremely tired of spending their time reviewing these types of mistakes when it is so easy to initially do what is expected of us. The minute you pick up a deposit, exit stage left, do not stop (don't speed either), and go straight to your brokerage/escrow and turn in the instrument. No going for coffee, no anything else—just turn it in, and you have fulfilled your obligations.

Please don't be preparing a defence for why you didn't do this. Seriously, what are you going to say? Also, do you really want all the pressure of worrying about what is going to happen, having your name published, having a permanent mark in your file, and attending courses, completing assignments and/or paying a fine? No, you don't, and there is absolutely no reason at all for any of these cases occurring.

If the deposit monies go anywhere other than the buyer's brokerage or whatever your legislation dictates, stop everything and gather up all the paperwork you will need. This is the one time you should be lazy (if that's what you want to call it) but smart and put the deposit monies in the buyers' brokerage/escrow as recommended. Come on; don't keep making these unnecessary and careless mistakes. Obey the rules and regulations in your market area.

On subject removals, if that's when you get the deposit, then you book an hour or whatever to pick it up and drive without stopping (except at red lights or stop signs ... oh, and for pedestrians) and go straight to your brokerage/escrow immediately. No more procrastinating—"Oh, I have time and will drop it off in the morning." Forget it, make this an automatic to-do. This is your simple four-step routine now after picking up any deposit monies:

1. Pick up the deposit.

2. Verify that the money is by way of bank draft, money order or however you specified it in the Contract of Purchase and Sale.

3. Verify that the deposit instrument is the correct date and amount, and has the proper payee name *(in trust).*

4. Take and give the monies to your brokerage/escrow if that is who will be holding the deposit.

Verify the above prior to leaving your buyers.

When deposit monies are received by you, no matter what you are doing, you stop everything and make sure they get submitted to your brokerage/escrow, if that is where it is going. No other options are open to you, okay? Make this a habit. If it really is inconvenient, then you call a courier and have it delivered immediately.

There are a few other deposit issues that colleagues have faced, so again, be very careful out there. The penalties for these were mainly suspensions, fines up to $1,000 and completing educational courses and/or educational assignments.

No one wants these types of problems, and they are often just mistakes or maybe lack of education. In some cases, it's just plain carelessness. Who in their right mind would want to pay the price for these mistakes? Follow your rules.

One day I sincerely hope that our authorities won't be hearing so many cases, but that is only possible if we as agents are more careful in preparing our contracts and remembering that this is a *very serious business*. Please, don't screw it up! I don't want to have to visit you in real estate jail. Remember, too, it is the public's money.

If you need some updating on the rules and regulations, all our authorities offer amazing courses, so do sign up for them. This is your professional career. Take good care of it.

Okay, now I am getting angry, because why is everyone having so much trouble with this? The above mistakes are not even close to the number of cases there have been, so something is wrong. Hopefully, the recap for deposits below will provide you with some assistance.

When you write your contract, you are going to put the deposits in the buyer's brokerage/escrow or where your legislation dictates. If this is not being done, stop everything and realize you need tons of paperwork and written disclosures to put it anywhere else. You may need to find your managing broker to help you, and if that is the case, do so.

You must offer independent/legal professional advice relating specifically to the deposits and how they are held. If need be, make it a subject.

You must explain in the contract that the buyers are aware of the ramifications of what could happen to their money—for example, if it went directly to the sellers, they will likely never see it again. If need be, make it a subject.

Statements Often Used for the Taking of Deposit Monies

Make sure you state how the deposit is to be taken. Bank draft or money order are the preferred methods. Certified cheques can be stopped, and most brokerages do not accept cash due to the money-laundering regulations.

Be careful if using bank wire transfer. When will it arrive in the trust account as required by your local authorities/regulators?

How and when deposits are due are often written using one of the following statements:

- *Upon Acceptance*

   Deposit to be $_____ by way of bank draft, money order *[or bank wire transfer]* upon acceptance of this contract by all parties.

- *Within 24 or 48 Hours of Acceptance*

  Deposit to be $_____ by way of bank draft, money
  order *[or bank wire transfer]* within *[24 or 48]* hours of acceptance
  of this contract by all parties.

- *Upon Removal of All Subjects*

  Deposit to be $_____ by way of bank draft, money
  order *[or bank wire transfer]* upon removal of all subjects.

- *24 or 48 Hours After Removal of All Subjects*

  Deposit to be $_____ by way of bank draft, money
  order *[or bank wire transfer]* *[24 or 48]* hours after removal of all
  subjects.

- *Increased After Removal of All Subjects*

  Deposit to be increased to $_____ by way of bank draft,
  money order *[or bank wire transfer]* upon removal of all subjects.

- *Increased 24 or 48 Hours after Removal of all Subjects*

  Deposit to be increased to $_____ by way of bank draft,
  money order *[or bank wire transfer]* within *[24 or 48]* hours upon
  removal of all subjects.

You must specify clearly when and by what method deposits are due. Diarize/instant-alert yourself the date to pick up the deposit, and book an hour of time minimum to allow you to deliver it to the specified party.

Never Ever Put a Date for When a Deposit Is Due

I have seen in the past number of months a huge problem created by writing deposits by way of bank draft by March 21, 20__. This date of March 21, 20__ corresponds to the date of removal of all subjects.

Here is what has happened and caused unbelievable grief for everyone.

Let's say you wrote the deposit to be by way of bank draft by March 21, 20__. This is *almost* the same as if you wrote the deposit to be by way of bank draft upon removal of all subject clauses, except that you specified a date the monies were due.

The contract was written on March 9, with the deposit payable on March 21, 20__. The buyers have the following clause or something similar in their contract.

Subject to the buyer entering into an unconditional agreement to sell the buyer's property at [address] by March 21, 20____. This subject is for the sole benefit of the buyer. However, the seller may, [select either <u>at any time</u> or upon receipt of another <u>acceptable</u> offer or <u>higher priced</u> offer], deliver a written notice to the buyer or to his or her representing <u>real estate Brokerage</u> and/ or representatives requiring the buyer to remove all conditions from the contract within [number of hours] of the delivery of the notice, not to include Saturdays, Sundays, and statutory holidays. If the buyer fails to remove all the conditions before the expiry of the notice period, the contract will terminate.

So here is the problem. You write the offer on March 9 with the deposit being paid on March 21, 20____. Now another offer appears, and the sellers invoke the above time clause. The buyers are prepared to remove all subjects, they really want this home, and so they go ahead and remove all subjects on March 13, but can you see the problem with the deposit? Since the contract was written with the deposit specifically due on March 21, the buyers can remove their subjects on March 13, but they do not have to increase the deposit monies until March 21, which is eight days later.

Oops! This is why you always want to state that the deposit is due upon removal of *all* subjects. Otherwise, everyone will be waiting until the deposit is actually received on March 21.

9. Deposits—If Any Interest Is Accrued

*The deposit is to be placed at interest and if any interest is accrued it will be for the benefit of the *[Sellers or Buyers]*.

Explanation

A deposit will not earn any interest if it is not written in the Contract of Purchase and Sale. If you put the above statement in your contracts and interest becomes beneficial for your buyers due to the amount of the deposit and/or the length of time the monies are in the trust account, then by using the words "if any" interest is accrued, you have obtained written authorization from all parties that interest can be paid. This is just a convenience if it became applicable, and it saves you doing an amendment to the original contract in order for one of the parties to receive any interest.

Please check with your brokerage as to their policies and procedures with respect to deposits earning interest.

10. Incorporation Of Documents

*Any and all documentation provided by the Sellers to the Buyers or the Buyers to the Sellers will be attached to, incorporated and form part of this Contract of Purchase and Sale.

Explanation

This is self-explanatory and saves you from having to remember to put the clause in for every separate disclosure, piece of paper or documentation received from one of the parties.

Remember to turn these documents in to your brokerage along with your contract and transaction record sheet.

11. Measurements/Room Sizes/Square Footage/Lot Size/Age

*The Buyers have been advised that if further information or exact measurements, square footage and/or lot size is a concern, the property should be independently measured and the Buyers should also make their own investigations as to the age of the buildings/structures. The Buyers are advised to verify the above information and arrange for any independent measurements and/or investigations at the earliest possible opportunity and in any event prior to proceeding with this Contract of Purchase and Sale.

All parties have been afforded the opportunity and advised to obtain independent Legal/Professional advice *[and have waived their right to put a subject in the Contract of Purchase and Sale]* and accept and are satisfied with the above possible concerns.

Explanation

Many have been using "that the buyers have measured and have had the opportunity to verify all measurements, square footage, etc.," and are satisfied with the same. Others have used something like "the buyers are aware all measurements are approximate." But there is absolutely no way these are going to hold up in a legal dispute. They are not specific enough, and we all know how many complaints there are over the square footage or age of a building in particular.

My statement is a combination of those from many of the boards in Canada, the USA and Australia, so remember that if you type it just once, you never have to retype it. Just copy and paste it or use one of my sample addendums already pretyped for you. (See appendix.)

The form itself is mainly for your file, and you can make a note of how you arrived at your calculations. It is better to be safe than sorry if there is any trouble in the future.

12. No Growth or Manufacture of Illegal Substances

*The Sellers warrant and guarantee that during the time the Sellers have owned the property, the use of the land/property/buildings and structures thereon have not been for the growth or manufacture of any illegal substances and that to the best of the Sellers knowledge the use of the land/property/buildings and structures thereon have never been for the growth or manufacture of illegal substances. This warranty shall survive and not merge on the completion of this transaction.

The [Sellers/Buyers or the Sellers and Buyers] have been afforded the opportunity and advised to seek independent Legal/Professional advice.

Explanation

This is self-explanatory. You have a duty to protect the public by using reasonable care and skill.

Important: If the sellers cross off the above wording or refuse to include the statement, then it will most likely be a material latent defect and will have to be disclosed separately in writing and prior to entering into a Contract of Purchase and Sale. See the chapter on material latent defects and the appendix.

13. Outstanding Orders

> *The Sellers warrant and guarantee there are no outstanding Work, Fire, Safety, Health or Environmental orders with any *[City/Municipal/Provincial/Governmental/Environmental]* Authorities/Regulators *[including the Strata Council, Strata Corporation and Property Management Companies if applicable]*.

Explanation

Years ago, my lawyer got very upset with me for not including the above statement in all my Contracts of Purchase and Sale. He actually threatened not to do anymore closings/conveyances for my clients if I didn't put this in every single contract. Obviously, he updated it recently to incorporate items we face today.

He explained that it protects everyone because what the sellers are saying is that up to and including the date they accept the contract, there have been no letters, notices, phone calls or orders from any governmental authorities telling them to do anything like remove a suite, upgrade the plumbing or electrical, obtain permits for renovations or bring the property up to fire codes.

I do know I might have thoughts about including this in a multiple-offer situation, as it could be a disadvantage to my buyers. However, I would make absolute certain that I had done my full due diligence, checked with every possible authority, and had the buyers personally check as well and sign a note attesting to that fact. I would explain this in full detail with the pros and cons of including or not including it and leave the final decision to the buyers.

I would personally be worried about leaving it out of the contract, but I would also worry it could cost them winning the bidding war. Whatever decision they make, I would document it in writing and even go so far as to have them sign they waived their right to include this statement, or did they want it included? It was their choice after I had explained the possible ramifications of including or omitting it.

Just a quick note here—whenever something has to be verified, whether it be zoning, the use of a property or the meanings on a Title Search, always try to have your clients personally confirm the specific items.

I have actually called to verify something and then someone else called and got told a different answer, so I am always extremely cautious. If possible, get a written reply to the concern. Often today, many authorities/governmental offices will not reply to e-mails, but they will correspond by fax. Be sure and check these items out and, if possible, obtain any and all information in writing. Err on the side of caution.

14. Plans/Permits/Documents/Drawings Will Be Supplied by the Sellers

*The Sellers warrant and guarantee to supply to the Buyers or the Buyers' Agents/Representatives/ Brokerage within *[3 calendar]* days of acceptance of this Contract of Purchase and Sale by all parties, at no cost to the Buyers, any blueprints, building plans, drawings, and/or other plans/permits/ documentation/correspondence and warranties applicable to the land/property/buildings and structures that are in the Sellers' possession.
The Sellers agree to allow access for any of these parties if required including those already agreed to in the Access for All Trades Statement.

Explanation

This is self-explanatory. You have a duty to protect the public by using reasonable care and skill.

15. Property Disclosure

*The Buyers have read, acknowledged and approved the attached Property Disclosure Statement which is incorporated into and forms part of this contract. The Buyers have been advised to seek independent Legal/Professional advice prior to entering into this contract.

Explanation

The subjects we use in most contracts often have the Property Disclosure Statement and the Title Search as subjects, but with the changes in our industry it is important for you to obtain these two documents prior to preparing an offer. This also means that your contract will have two fewer subjects.

The above statement has the Property Disclosure Statement incorporated and forming part of the contract, so you do not have to worry about adding it in when you write an offer. You will have it already included and won't have to think about it.

Some sellers may cross it off, since they may not want it incorporated, but that will be sorted during the negotiations.

Note to Listing Agents

Hand out or e-mail the Title Search and Property Disclosure whenever a colleague inquires about the property. Make your job easier and be efficient. If you are the listing agent, hand out the Property Disclosure and Title Search to everyone or e-mail it to anyone calling on your listing. If this is not possible, at least give it to the buyers' agents when they first show the property.

There are a number of reasons to do this—including that it will meet the requirements of disclosure and other various rules our authorities and/or our legislation expect us to follow. Remember, the main purpose of our authorities is to protect the public, and if we want to keep our real estate license, we must comply no matter what we think or how we feel about the rules and regulations or the legislation.

There are obviously different rules in different locations, but your job is to protect everyone, and disclosure is the safest way to go, even if it is not necessarily legislated or contained in your regulations. Seriously, you are far safer just to disclose everything you can and know about, with your clients' lawful and preferably written instructions. These disclosures protect everyone, including you. The sooner the better is always the safest course.

Distribute and/or obtain the Property Disclosure Statement as soon as possible so everyone knows if there are any items that may need written acknowledgement prior to entering into a contract. Now all agents will be in full compliance.

I know a number of agents who say you cannot have the Property Disclosure Statement until there is an accepted offer. But it is best if the sellers disclose everything that may affect the buyers in advance rather than waiting until there is an offer on the table. Not only that, many disclosure items have to be acknowledged in writing prior to entering into a Contract of Purchase and Sale, so if they are a subject or not dealt with in advance, you are not in compliance.

Why would anyone want to go through the entire process of writing, presenting and coming to an agreed contract only to have it fall apart due to some undisclosed condition that affects the buyers' decision to purchase the property? Disclosure is always the safest course.

Remember, too, the Property Disclosure is only the sellers' *awareness* of items, to the best of their knowledge.

Sample Discipline Cases

An agent failed to use reasonable care and skill when providing the brokerage with a Property Disclosure Statement that had not been signed by both the buyers and sellers. By this oversight of not obtaining signatures on the Property Disclosure Statement, the agent's/rep's name was published for all to see, there was now a permanent mark in this individual's file, and a lot of time and trouble went into replying to the charge.

All of this emotional stress and hours of preparing a defence was because of failure to double-check for signatures. This was either just plain sloppiness or carelessness. It really isn't worth it, is it? Always double-check your paperwork. The onus of proof is on you.

16. Referral Fee Disclosure

*The *[Sellers/Buyers or the Sellers and Buyers]* acknowledge having received and signed a Disclosure of Referral Fees or *[other incentive/bonus points if applicable]* in accordance with the *[your Act or your Authorities/Regulators]* before the presentation of this Contract of Purchase and Sale.

17. Remuneration Disclosure

*The *[Sellers/Buyers or the Sellers and Buyers]* acknowledge having received and signed a Disclosure of Remuneration in accordance with the *[your Act or your Authorities/Regulators]* before the presentation of this Contract of Purchase and Sale. The *Sellers/Buyers or the Sellers and Buyers]* have been afforded the opportunity and advised to seek independent Legal/Professional advice.

Explanation

This is self-explanatory. We know our authorities require that we disclose to our clients any referral fees and remuneration we will receive or anticipate receiving prior to entering into a contract. Don't forget that if, for example, a client uses a particular bank and you receive bonus points to obtain prizes, this must also be disclosed. All monies, including bonuses that we receive, must be received through our respective brokerages.

True Story

My fantastic mortgage broker will sometimes send me a coffee gift certificate at Christmas as a thank-you for any business I may have referred to him. I must make this disclosure known to my clients. If buyers asked me for his name and I gave it to them, I would also give a written note stating that if they use him, I may receive a gift certificate at Christmas for coffee. I would also include the possible (anticipated) amount of the dollar value it may be.

Sample Discipline Cases

An agent and/or brokerage committed professional misconduct:

- by altering the commission to be paid by the sellers without the initials of the sellers before delivering the contracts to the brokerage, and failing to inform the brokerage that he held a percentage of shares of the said sellers.

- by accepting remuneration directly from the sellers or from someone other than the brokerage he was licensed with.

- by accepting remuneration from someone other than his brokerage.

- by not disclosing to the buyers his actual commission and that, while acting as a limited dual agent, he failed to accurately disclose to the buyers that the agent had reduced the commission by X amount of dollars.

- by failing to disclose in writing to the buyer the remuneration the agent anticipated receiving for providing real estate services.

- by failing to disclose to the buyer that the agent paid a referral fee of X amount of dollars concerning this transaction to the wife of a person acting under power of attorney for the buyer.

- while acting as a limited dual agent by failing to disclose the total amount he would be receiving from the sellers.

- by accepting X amount of dollars in relation to real estate services directly from the seller, by way of a cheque.

- by failing to disclose to the buyers and the brokerage the source of the remuneration, the amount of the remuneration, or the method of calculation of the remuneration.

- by completing the Disclosure of Remuneration forms showing X Brokerage as the agent's/rep's brokerage when in fact X Brokerage was representing the sellers.

- by failing to disclose to the clients involved in those transactions the remuneration the agent would be receiving in connection with the transaction.

- by failing to promptly and fully disclose a conflict of interest arising from her provision of a gift of X amount of dollars for use as part of the down payment for the purchase.

- by failing to disclose to the buyers the amount and source of the remuneration the agent expected to receive.

- by accepting remuneration directly from the seller in relation to an agreement between him and the seller that the listing contract for the property would be cancelled.

This is just a very small sampling of the number of discipline cases our authorities had to review. Why are there so many cases when we all know that we must disclose this information?

I am hoping that by having the two above statements in all of your contracts, that will at least remind you to always predisclose these items, and it will not be a continuing problem.

18. Registering in Another Name [Do Not Use "and/or Nominee"]

---

*For good and valuable consideration the Sellers and Buyers mutually agree that the Buyers can assign their rights under this Contract of Purchase and Sale and the agreement formed by its acceptance by all parties. The Buyers acknowledge and guarantee that such assignment would not in any way affect their obligations to complete the terms and conditions of this Contract of Purchase and Sale including their obligation to pay the purchase monies to the Sellers.
[Beware of the problems with the Financial Institutions].

Explanation

Do not ever use the words "and/or Nominee" or "and/or Assignee." It could negate your Contract of Purchase and Sale due to uncertainty.

If ever you receive a contract with these words on it, usually inserted beside the buyer's names, you must immediately cross them off and have them initialled. Remember to also check if these words appear on what I call the "action page" of the contract, where the sellers and buyers sign as well. Now you have a counter-offer no matter what. This is just what we do not want to do. Use the above clause or something similar that your authorities recommend.

If you have buyers demanding these words, explain to them that the way to handle this is to add in the above statement. Remember, too, that banks and financial institutions have been creating some problems by demanding that if the contract is going to be registered in another name, they want the contract rewritten in that specific name.

The courts could and may elect to decide that the contract is unenforceable due to the uncertain identity of the buyers if you use "and/or Nominee" or "and/or Assignee." Each area will have its own legislation regarding this and cases to support or not support the argument above. In British Columbia, Canada, residential contracts from our authorities do not have any wording in the prewritten agreement preventing a buyer from assigning or registering in another name. You must check with your own authorities and legislation.

There are always times when the normal rule will not apply, and that would be in a court-ordered sale (foreclosure or otherwise). The name of the buyers cannot easily be changed once the court enters the order for the sale. Therefore, you could not use the above statement.

Suggestion: In a court-ordered sale, make sure you use the full legal name of your buyers and state if they are registering as joint tenants or tenants in common. This is obviously critical to your buyers. Again, it cannot easily be changed once the courts award the contract.

Remember to attach proof of signing authority to all your documents if they are registering, for example, in a company name. You must always attach proof of signing authority to all your documents and turn it into your brokerage with your transaction.

If the seller is financing the buyer or the sale is court-ordered, you cannot use the above clause.

Signing on Behalf of Your Clients

Because signing on behalf of your clients is important, I will briefly review it here. It is not included in the statements in most contracts, but it is so very serious that I will give you a quick overview about signing on behalf of your clients or acting on their verbal instructions.

I have always wondered why anyone would take the risk of initialling or signing for their clients. It is just too dangerous, and more importantly, do you have the proper written authority from them to act on their behalf? In the appendix, I have attached a sample form that you could use to obtain prior written authorization to act on their behalf. See "Signing on Behalf of Your Clients/Customers."

You must have their written authority/authorization *before* you ever begin to act on their behalf. Our authorities in British Columbia are very strict with the enforcement of these types of issues, and I agree that they should be. Do not ever convey to the sellers or buyers that you, for example, have an accepted Contract of Purchase and Sale if you do not have the authorized signatures or initials required to enforce the contract.

The parties could appoint someone, whether it is a real estate agent or another person, to represent them and sign as their representative. This would meet the requirements that real estate must be in writing. This appointment of someone must also be very specific, setting out the exact terms and conditions.

A fax is acceptable, but whatever written authority you receive must be in your hands *prior* to you acting as their agent. You'll need the licensee's signature as agent for [Sellers/Buyers name] followed by the date, time and your full brokerage name.

Sample Discipline Cases

A colleague committed professional misconduct because he did not confirm that the executor had the authority to sign the contract. He also forgot to mention that the estate had not received Letters Probate and therefore he did not have the authority to transfer the title. His penalty was suspension for approximately one week, a fine of $1,000 and the completion of educational courses.

Here are a few more examples. An agent and/or brokerage failed:

- by permitting someone other than the client to sign a contract without written authority or without an executed power of attorney.

- to ensure that the Contracts of Purchase and Sale were signed by the seller or a person legally authorized to sign on the seller's behalf, and failing to ensure that one or more of the sellers' signatures on the documents was witnessed.

- to apply reasonable care and skill in drafting the letter whereby the buyer authorized the agent "to sign on their behalf on small changes to a Contract of Purchase and Sale" and failed to include the property address and time frame for which this authority was granted.

- to act in the best interest of the buyer and acted outside of the scope of his authority in that he signed on behalf of the buyer to remove all subjects for the purchase of the property, which is not a "small change" to a Contract of Purchase and Sale.

- to ensure that the documents requiring the signature of the seller were in fact signed by the seller.

- by creating a replacement contract by signing and initialling the sellers' signatures and initials without the sellers' knowledge or consent.

- by initialling a change of completion date on behalf of the seller without written authorization to do so.

- by signing the MLS® Listing Contract Amendment Forms with a signature similar to the client's signature, without the client's authorization.

- by not obtaining a second buyer's signature on an addendum.

- by allowing a client to sign the listing agreement and contract as seller without verifying his identity or his purported ownership interest in the property, and allowing the client to sign the name of the seller on the listing agreement and contract knowing this individual was not the seller and that the signature as written was false and misleading.

A managing broker was suspended for one year for not taking reasonable steps to respond to a client's allegation that an agent had forged the client's signatures, failing to undertake an adequate level of investigation of the client's complaint, and failing to impose sufficient remedial measures on the agent given that the agent acknowledged the forgery of the client's signatures. The broker was found to have demonstrated incompetence by not advising the agent of the requirements of having authorization to sign on behalf of a client before signing a contract; failed to be actively engaged in the management of the brokerage ensuring business of the brokerage was carried out competently; and provided an inadequate level of supervision for related associate brokers and representatives

Now, back to the statements that could be in most of your Contracts of Purchase and Sale.

19. Residents

*The Sellers hereby declare that they are Residents of *[_____]* as defined under the Income Tax Act.

20. Returning of the Sellers' Documents

*In the event this transaction does not complete, the Buyers warrant and guarantee to return to the Sellers or the Sellers/Sellers' Agents/Representatives/Brokerage all documents/plans and Disclosures that the Buyers have received from the Sellers, within [3 calendar] days of the Sellers and Buyers signing an Unconditional Cancellation/Release.

Explanation

These are self-explanatory.

21. Sellers Agree to Allow Time for Buyers to Remove Subjects

> *For good and valuable consideration of [One Dollar $1.00 or $_____] given by the Buyers and hereby acknowledged and received by the Sellers, the Sellers hereby warrant and guarantee that their acceptance of this offer will not be withdrawn or revoked prior to the date for all subjects to be removed.
> [Seal]
> Time shall remain of the essence.
> *[Type the word [Seal] exactly as shown]*.

Explanation

The above statement is also known as an Option Clause. There are many sophisticated buyers who will demand that you put in what can be called a "whim and fancy" subject or an "iffy" subject. A very simple example is "subject to satisfactory financing" or "subject to finalization of the preapproved mortgage," or "subject to the buyer obtaining satisfactory insurance." None of these are very specific or definitive; the courts have enforced them at times and at other times they have not enforced them. Real estate is not always straightforward or black and white.

The usage of the above option clause is a very controversial issue, and I will give you the facts and details of an incident in our market area and leave the final decision of what to do to you.

Here is what happened: The sellers received Offer #1 of $300,000 "subject to satisfactory financing," and by the way, it also said "subject to arranging insurance satisfactory to the buyers." I would think that is also a so-called "whim and fancy" or "iffy" subject.

Anyhow, the sellers accepted the offer with five days for removal of all subjects, and those subjects were for the sole benefit of the buyers. Now, remember, Contracts of Purchase and Sale are signed under "seal" and state this or something similar in the preprinted wording:

> **Acceptance Irrevocable**
> The contract states that it is executed under seal and therefore the seller cannot revoke the offer during the period prior to the date specified for the buyer to either:
> * Fulfill or waive the terms and conditions herein contained;
> * And/or exercise any options herein contained.

To most of us, this means that the sellers will give the buyers time to fulfill, remove or waive any and all subjects, but this was not the case in this true story. The sellers received Offer #2 the next day of $330,000, and of course they wanted to take that offer. Offer #2 was $30,000 more than Offer #1.

They raced to their lawyer, who told them that even though it was signed under seal and stated that they had to give the buyers time to remove, fulfill or waive their subjects, they did not have to do so in this case. Why? The sellers' lawyer explained that the real estate agents did not make clearly definitive subjects, and so the sellers could accept Offer #2. The subjects were too vague to be enforced, and get this: It was also because of the wording for the subject that said "satisfactory insurance." The sellers were thrilled; they were going to get $30,000 more!

The buyers were upset and angry, and they stormed off to their own lawyer for advice. The buyers' lawyer agreed with the sellers' lawyer and said, "I am sorry, but the subjects just are not specific enough, including the insurance subject being satisfactory to the buyers, and so you lose. The sellers can take the higher offer of $330,000."

This never went to the courts that I know of, but I am amazed it didn't. I was quite shocked, because I too relied on the "Acceptance Irrevocable" that is preprinted in most Contracts of Purchase and Sale.

I am overly cautious and did try to get some advice on this, and a few lawyers other than the above two lawyers involved in this incident told me that as a double protection, one should always add in the Option Clause if they have "whim and fancy" or "iffy" subjects.

I remember doing this many years ago, but it was often only when there was a very long subject removal date, for rezoning or something similar. There was also a very large deposit taken. I did decide one thing personally: I would always include the Option Clause in any Contract of Purchase and Sale that I wrote in the future if I was working for my clients. It has not been tested to my knowledge, but I do know if I was representing a buyer, on the advice of a number of lawyers I would insert it as a precaution.

I strongly urge you to verify this with legal authorities in your market area. If you are advised to include it in your statements in most contracts as a precautionary backup, then you must make sure that the one dollar is paid and you obtain a receipt. No sense doing it halfway.

If you are going to take this route, please make sure it's done correctly. Check with your legal people or authorities. I have asked numerous lawyers and have been told that it would not hurt to include it, especially with the case mentioned above. Others say it is not necessary, as it is already included in the preprinted wording in our contracts.

My question then is, why was the seller allowed to dismiss the original offer and not allow the buyers time to remove their subjects? I don't honestly know the answer. The legal advice I obtained varies.

I did leave the above Option Clause in the statements that could be in most contracts so that it would always be there just in case you did put a "whim and fancy" or "iffy" subject and may not remember to include the clause, but again, please obtain your own independent legal and professional advice for your market area. Don't forget to pay the one dollar and get a receipt if you decide to use it.

22. Sellers Have Disclosed Material Latent Defects

*The Sellers warrant and guarantee that there are no Material Latent Defects as defined under their [Acts/Legislation/Authorities/Regulators] and if there are they warrant and guarantee they have been disclosed separately in writing to the Buyers and the Buyers acknowledge receipt of and accept this Disclosure prior to entering into this Contract of Purchase and Sale of any and all Material Latent Defects regarding the condition and maintenance or any other items that could affect the land/property/buildings and structures including items designated lawfully or defined as Material Latent Defects [under your Acts/Legislation/Authorities/Regulators].
The [Sellers/Buyers or the Sellers and Buyers] have been afforded the opportunity and advised to seek independent Legal/Professional advice]
[The disclosure, if any, will be attached to, incorporated and form part of this Contract of Purchase and Sale].
[This warranty shall survive and not merge on the completion of this transaction]?

Explanation

Stigmatized Properties

Let's take a look at stigmatized properties first. These are items that could potentially affect buyers in their decision of whether to purchase a property or not. They deal with issues that have no actual physical effect on a property.

Stigmatized properties may have issues associated with them that could have a psychological impact. Maybe there is a circumstance that occurred in or near the property but does not affect the functioning of the property itself. A few examples that buyers may be concerned with are:

- rumours that the house is haunted

- a death occurred in the property

- a sexual offender is reported living nearby or across the street

- the previous tenant/owner was reported on the news as being a member of a gang or charged with a serious crime

- the property was vandalized and/or robbed three times in the past year.

If there was a death in the property, would it make a difference if it was a pet, an elderly family member brought home to receive loving care, or a murder? These examples illustrate how difficult it is to clearly define what a stigmatized property might be. What one person might find unacceptable may be of little or no importance to another.

If disclosure is mandatory in your market area, then obviously, you would disclose; but if not, be careful if buyers tell you they do not want, for example, a property that is reportedly haunted. This then becomes your responsibility to inquire and verify. It now becomes an issue of possible required disclosure.

In British Columbia, Canada, we do not have to disclose stigmatized properties in the same way we must disclose material latent defects. Other market areas must always disclose stigmatized properties along with material latent defects. As already mentioned, disclosure is always the safest method, but there are times when a seller may not want to make such disclosures since they feel it may affect the final sale price of their property.

Material Latent Defects

Material latent defect means a defect that cannot be discerned through a reasonable inspection of the property. Agents are having a difficult time understanding the obligations of disclosure; this includes how and when the disclosure has to be made.

In our market area, material latent defects must be disclosed separately in writing prior to entering into a Contract of Purchase and Sale. Most other market areas seem to be very similar with their requirements of disclosure.

Our regulations state that the sellers must make disclosure, and if they do not then the onus of disclosure falls to the listing agent. If the sellers demanded you not disclose, these are not lawful instructions, and you would have to educate your sellers why these defects must be disclosed. If need be, your managing broker or your legal/professional council could assist in explaining this to the sellers.

How do you know what has to be disclosed? After all my research and finally comprehending the requirements of disclosure, I have found that the easiest way might be for you to take a look at what your local disclosure requirements are and then, when you are ready to write an offer, review the list and see if the property your buyers are looking at has any material latent defects or stigmas.

Requirements for Disclosure

A material latent defect includes a defect that renders the real estate dangerous or potentially dangerous to the occupants, unfit for habitation, or unfit for the purpose for which a party is acquiring it, if the party has made this purpose known to the licensee, or the licensee has otherwise become aware of this purpose.

This could include a grow operation, an illegal drug operation, mold or hazardous environmental issues; it may be anything that causes the property to be dangerous to the new buyers depending on who occupied it in previous years. Another problem might be wiring so old it could cause a fire. Or let's say your buyers told you they do not want to buy a property where a death occurred in the home, and you are now aware of this requirement that originally was what we called a stigma and has now possibly become a material latent defect.

One buyer told her agent that she wanted to run a beauty salon out of the house she was buying, but the agent sold her a property without obtaining disclosure that the zoning was residential use only and therefore it was unfit for the purpose the buyer was acquiring it. Disclosure should have been made.

Disclosure is also required for a defect that would involve a great expense to remedy. A "great expense" could be $100 to one person and $1,000 to another. Disclose and be very careful with this requirement.

You are also required to disclose a situation in which a local government or other local authority has given a notice to the client or the agent indicating that a circumstance must or should be remedied. This could be where the government or other authorities have told the sellers to bring the plumbing or wiring up to code, or to shut down an unauthorized suite.

This is part of the reason why, in your statements that could be in most contracts, I have included the clause stating that the sellers warrant there are no outstanding orders. They are confirming that there have been no letters, notices, phone calls or orders from any governmental authorities telling them to remove a suite, upgrade the plumbing or electrical, etc. This acknowledgement is only up to and including the date of acceptance of the contract by all parties.

This could also be applicable for strata titled properties. The sellers would be confirming that they have not received any notices from the strata council, property-management company or other authorities to remove, for example, the hardwood flooring, or enclose the opened-up loft area, or change any other items done without approvals or permits.

A lack of appropriate municipal building and other permits is the item that triggers disclosure for most of us. "Lack of permits" relates to any renovations without permits, plumbing and electrical without permits, and more particularly unauthorized accommodation or illegal suites, including where a garage has been converted without permits or a loft area opened up in a strata unit.

When to Make the Disclosure

The sellers are required to disclose any and all material latent defects (and stigmas in some market areas) separately in writing prior to entering into a Contract of Purchase and Sale. Disclosure of all known material latent defects (stigmas) must be provided to the buyer before any agreement for the acquisition or disposition of the real estate is entered into.

The timing of the disclosure is critical. Material latent defects must be disclosed separately in writing prior to entering into a Contract of Purchase and Sale. This is why we are asking for the Property Disclosure upfront. If the sellers have filled it in, then the buyers would hopefully have disclosure prior to entering into a contract and in writing. The agents must remember to cross-reference receipt of this predisclosure in the contract, which is accomplished by using the above statement.

Here in British Columbia, disclosures of material latent defects can be made on the Property Disclosure. The sellers must use initials, and don't *you* ever fill in the disclosure form for them. They can disclose on a separate piece of paper or on the form "Material Latent Defects | Disclosure," as long as it is signed and dated by the sellers and the buyers prior to entering into a contract.

The other problem agents face is that owners may not sign the Property Disclosure and cross it off or state they never lived in the property. Trustees, referral companies, executors and the like often have their own Schedule A or disclaimer of the property being sold "as is and where is," and they will not warrant or guarantee anything; or they have a statement that they say must be incorporated into the Contract of Purchase and Sale stating that they are selling the property "as is and where is" and won't guarantee or disclose knowledge of anything.

You, as their agent, cannot contract out of our laws, regulations, or legislation. You must disclose if you know. So how are you going to handle this? It is difficult to explain to these types of sellers, but you must make them aware of the laws. Check your area.

You could ask the owners to write, for example, renovations done without permits, or unauthorized/illegal accommodation, or whatever the material latent defect is, on the Property Disclosure in the remarks section, even if they crossed off the rest of the disclosure. If not, they could just disclose it on the form "Material Latent Defects | Disclosure" in the appendix of this book, on a form you have, or on a piece of paper. They could also just hand-write it on their Schedule A if it was a trustee/referral company, something like "Property contains unauthorized accommodation or renovations done without permits," and have your buyers sign and date it prior to entering into a contract.

You as their agent should put in the REALTOR® remarks that there is a material latent defect and advise other agents to get the written disclosure prior to writing an offer. In some areas, this should also be on the schedule attached to your listing agreement. This means everything will be in compliance, because disclosure will have been made prior to entering into a Contract of Purchase and Sale. This is why it is really smart if you hand out the Property Disclosure along with the Title Search in advance. Maybe you could also post it online or whatever is the easiest possible way for other agents to receive this information.

A number of agents have asked if the buyers couldn't just initial or sign (remember, signatures are always stronger than initials) beside the disclosure in the MLS® printout. The problem you may face is that this information is often only in the full REALTOR® printout, not the *public* printout. The buyer's agent could just write it on the *public* printout, which often shows the remuneration you are receiving unless you are in Limited Dual. (See the form "Material Latent Defects | Disclosure" in the appendix.)

So there are lots of ways to handle this, but you must find the easiest solution for you as an agent. Some boards have the Property Disclosure and Title Search in a drop-down box along with the listing information. At least you can then get the disclosures and documents prior to entering into a Contract of Purchase and Sale. Other agents have told me they are posting the information on their website so it is easily accessible, and there are those who have made it a habit to e-mail both the Property Disclosure and Title Search to everyone calling on the property, and they also have copies in their files to hand out at any showings and open houses. They also distribute other required disclosures at the same time.

You need to work together on this and maybe even with your local boards to help you fulfill your legal duties. We have so much predisclosure and paperwork these days, so let's find a way to make it much simpler to do business professionally but conveniently and easily.

The form "Material Latent Defects | Disclosure" could also be filled in and completed by your buyers if you cannot get the required disclosure in advance from the listing agents/ sellers. What you would do is have the buyers sign it, put it on top of your Contract of Purchase and Sale, and have the sellers sign it prior to viewing the contract to be on the safe side. It must be signed prior to entering into a contract. This would work. Your buyers have already signed the disclosure.

If you read, or when touring the property you noticed, there was an unauthorized accommodation, renovations without permits, or other possible material latent defects, then you could go with this format, although it would just be so easy and fantastic if the listing agents would send it to you the day you initially phone and inquire about the property.

How to Make the Disclosure

Disclosure must be separate from the Contract of Purchase and Sale in writing and can be:

- on a piece of paper signed and dated by all parties including on the MLS® *public* printout

- on the Property Disclosure Statement signed and dated by all parties

- on the form "Material Latent Defects | Disclosure" signed and dated by all parties.

This is why we are now asking for the Property Disclosure Statement upfront. If the sellers have completed it, then any disclosures will hopefully have been made and can be acknowledged as per our regulations. If we make the Property Disclosure Statement a subject and then receive it after a contract has been entered into, it does not meet the requirements of full written disclosure prior to entering into a Contract of Purchase and Sale.

When you are going to show a property, always ask the listing agent if there are any disclosures that must be made should your buyers decide to make an offer. See if you can get these in advance and make your life much easier.

In the appendix, I have included a form to help you when you call a listing agent prior to writing an offer: "Questionnaire to Listing Agents | Prior to Writing an Offer." This is a convenient checklist for you to use and remember to ask the right questions. For convenience and when you are ready to write an offer, there is a second form called "Questionnaire to Listing Agents | Ready to Write an Offer."

The listing agents do not have to give you answers to these questions, but they may have received permission from the sellers to provide you with some of the answers. Both these questionnaires are of value to the sellers as well as the buyers. If the listing agents give you any answers to the questions—such as preferred completion, possession and adjustment dates, and that the stove in the basement is not included—it will likely limit counter-offers. Try to obtain everything you can upfront and early on in the process.

Remember, too, if the sellers cross off the entire Property Disclosure Statement, stating that they have never lived in the property or for another particular reason, they can still write the words in the remarks that "the property contains unauthorized accommodation" as an example and hand this out to everyone viewing the property so they have it prior to entering into a contract. This works.

If the sellers refuse to make the required disclosure, then the onus of disclosure falls on the agent. If the sellers further instruct the agent to withhold a required disclosure, the agent must refuse to provide further trading services to or on behalf of that client. This is the time for the agent to find the managing broker or legal council for advice. No one wants to give up a listing unless it is absolutely necessary.

Our duty of confidentiality does not allow us to withhold known material facts about the condition of the sellers' property from the buyer, or to misrepresent the property's condition. If we did so, this could possibly constitute misrepresentation and impose liability on the sellers and agents/brokerage.

A few examples of items that could possibly be classed as material latent defects that the sellers/listing agents may have to make are:

- unauthorized accommodation

- illegal suites

- anything without the required permits

- stigmatized properties (could possibly become material latent defects)

- plumbing problems

- PCB Pipes

- structural issues

- aluminum wiring

- grow-ops, labs, etc. (could be hazardous, cause mold or other environmental issues, and may even fall into the category of being dangerous or potentially dangerous to the occupants depending on the previous occupants)

- mold

- buried oil tanks

- electromagnetic fields (some buyers have felt these are or could be dangerous or potentially dangerous to the occupants)

- strata assessments

- renovations without strata approval

- other strata lots have leaked and the owners know because of a building envelope study and council asks for an engineering firm to confirm. If the sellers know about significant building deficiencies, whether confirmed or under investigation, they must disclose the problems to buyers.

This list is not all-encompassing. Please seek independent legal/professional advice if further information/clarification is required.

If you answer yes to any of the following, then disclosure is most likely needed.

- Is anything in the property dangerous?

- Is it unfit for habitation?

- Is it unfit for the reason the buyers are buying the property?

- Is anything going to be a major expense? (Remember, this could be just $100 to some.)

- Has any authority told the sellers to remedy the property, upgrade the plumbing or wiring, shut part of the property down, etc.?

- Do they have permits for everything?

True Story

A property was listed for over 2.5 million dollars and had just been "busted" as a grow-op that day. It was on the front page of all the newspapers and on the news.

The agent had the seller sign a piece of paper that the property was "busted" as a grow-op, and there was no electricity in the outbuildings. The seller then put the date on it so this piece of paper met with the disclosure requirements of being in writing. She could have signed the Property Disclosure, used the Material Latent Defect form, used a piece of paper (which is what she did) and even signed and dated one of the newspaper articles. (I often wonder if the seller signed the disclosure behind bars.)

The agent was very experienced and careful when writing any contract and followed the rules, so she gave this disclosure out in advance and had the buyers sign and date it.

Rumour had it that the buyers were absolutely okay with the disclosure and kept talking about it. My red flag went up immediately. Why on earth would the buyers be making this claim? It just didn't make sense. I asked to review the file that day and realized why the buyers were okay with all this. Can you guess why?

Banks can often be difficult when lending on these types of properties, and today insurance companies are the same. Their rules have changed, and an agent should always be offering a subject to obtaining insurance.

The agent made a simple mistake that could have been an absolute disaster had the transaction proceeded to completion. She forgot to cross-reference receipt of the material latent defect in the Contract of Purchase and Sale. She just went too fast while preparing the contract and being bullied by the buyers. She just missed including it. Had she used the above suggested 32 statements that could be in most of your contracts, she would not have forgotten to cross-reference receipt of the disclosure of the defect.

I worry when these things happen and try to pretend it is happening to me, so how could I get out of this mess? Thank goodness the whole transaction fell apart. I was very relieved and could sleep again.

I knew this could be very serious with our authorities, so I did follow up and asked what would have happened to the agent had this closed and then the bank and insurance company found out about it. The authorities said it could have been construed as committing fraud. Fraud just didn't enter my mind. It was an honest mistake that the agent just forgot to do this.

It was an oversight, especially since the buyers were bullying the agent and yakking a mile a minute while she was preparing the contract. These buyers were the type who knew everything about real estate—or so they thought.

You do not get a second chance if you make a mistake. The written wording you used will supersede your best intentions. This just proves you have to double- or triple-check every contract, no matter what. Always cross-reference any separate documents that were received in the contract. You can see how serious it can be if you do forget. If you are using the 32 statements that could be in most of your Contracts of Purchase and Sale and the other recommended clauses, phrases and subjects, this won't happen to you. You will not forget.

Sample Discipline Cases

You will see from the samples below that just one simple error or mistake can lead to a number of possible reprimands. The actual failure to disclose a material latent defect led to other violations as explained below. Take your time and make sure whatever information you or your clients provide is accurate and truthful. You have a duty to research simple rumours of neighbours or others and follow up and disclose if necessary.

Don't mess with this. It is so much stress to prepare your defence, to have your name and mistake published, and to attend a hearing which is formal and definitely not a good experience. Seriously, take your time and be very careful. Research everything. The onus is on you.

- One agent did not confirm there was an electrical-inspection certificate when offering a mobile home for sale. The lack of this certificate is considered a material latent defect and therefore should have been disclosed in writing prior to entering into a Contract of Purchase and Sale. This led to untrue or misleading representations in the data input sheet. Penalty: suspended for approximately three weeks, a fine of $1,000 and completion of educational courses.

- Another colleague failed to disclose that one suite was non-conforming and that building or occupancy permits were not in place. This led to published advertising containing false statements or misrepresentations that the agent knew or should have known were untrue. Penalty: suspended for approximately two weeks, a fine of $750, completion of educational assignments and completion of a number of educational courses.

- An agent did not disclose his relationship with the sellers to the buyers and did not disclose the missing approvals for work that had been done. Because of this, he failed to secure approvals he knew or ought to have known were required. Penalty: suspended for approximately two weeks, a fine of $750 and completion of educational courses.

- A colleague advised the sellers to answer no to the question on the Property Disclosure Statement that says, "Are you aware if the premises or property have been used as a marijuana grow operation or to manufacture illegal drugs?" He failed to disclose to the buyers that the sellers had used the house and garage as a marijuana grow operation; he also failed to disclose to the buyers that the sellers had grown marijuana plants outside the house. By not disclosing the above, he did not ensure that the buyers could make any further enquiries; he also personally failed to make any further enquiries or confirm any rumours. Penalty: suspended for approximately one week, a fine of $1,250 and completion of a remedial education course.

Here are a few more examples. In these cases, an agent and/or brokerage failed:

- to advise buyers to make further inquiries and be satisfied regarding the extent of the electrical issues.

- to use reasonable efforts to find out if the seller had obtained the necessary permit to construct a wall and to ask if it complied with the bylaws.

- to use reasonable care and skill by not recommending to the buyers that the Contract of Purchase and Sale of the property be made subject to the buyers receiving and being satisfied with a written report from the company engaged to remove the vermiculite from the property and that the vermiculite had been removed.

Think of the stress of facing these types of inquiries and the time you will spend preparing your case and attending any hearings ordered. Also, how much paperwork is going to be required, including providing copies of every piece of paper relating to the contract?

Most discipline hearings are unnecessary, because they are often the result of a simple lack of knowledge, experience, or care. The amount of business you lose while defending yourself could be substantial, as you are concentrating on a mistake that you most likely could have avoided.

When you are unsure if something is a required disclosure, look at your rules and see if it applies to the item you are questioning. When in doubt, disclose. Make certain your sellers are aware of this. Remember, stigmatized properties could possibly be classed as material latent defects, and in some market areas disclosure is mandatory of any stigma. If you hear rumours or are concerned about anything, *anything at all*, you have a duty to make further inquiries and protect your clients.

I have also realized that I should carry copies of the "Material Latent Defect | Disclosure" form with me to every appointment. I never want to be caught unprepared on a topic that comes up so frequently when preparing an offer. You could also just have this on your computer if that is what you use.

23. Sellers Hereby Authorize Buyers to Obtain Documents and Information
[This Puts the Buyers in the Sellers' Shoes]

*The Sellers hereby authorize the Buyers/Buyers' Agents/Representatives/Brokerage/Legal/ Professional Representatives/Agents to view, inspect and obtain copies of any and all the records, correspondence, documents including but not limited to information that may be on record in the [your Authorities/Regulators/Governmental Agencies including Strata Corporations/Councils/ Property Managers if applicable] offices with respect to the said land/property/buildings/ structures at no cost to the Sellers.
The Sellers agree to allow access for any of these parties if required including those already agreed to in the Access for All Trades Statement.

24. Sellers Will Sign Necessary Documentation and Allow Access

*The Sellers warrant and guarantee to sign/authorize any applications/documentation required from any *[City/Municipal/Governmental/your Authorities/Regulators]* and/or any other trades/ sources necessary at no cost to the Sellers for the Buyers/Buyers' Agents/Representatives/ Brokerage to obtain any further information/documentation.
The Sellers agree to allow access for any of these parties if required including those already agreed to in the Access for All Trades Statement.

25. Separate Disclosures | Statements

*The Buyers/Sellers acknowledge having received and signed a *[_____]* *[prior to entering into this Contract of Purchase and Sale]* which is incorporated and forms part of this Contract of Purchase and Sale.

26. Survey

*If the Sellers have a Survey they will give it to the Buyers or the Buyers' Agents/Representatives/ Brokerage within *[3 calendar]* days of acceptance of this Contract of Purchase and Sale by all parties and at no cost to the Buyers. The Sellers warrant and guarantee no additions, alterations or changes have been made including to the land/property/buildings and structures, fences and/ or improvements since the date of the Survey *[which will be attached to, incorporated and form part of this contract]*.

27. Taxes | Accounting/Professional Advice

*The *[Sellers/Buyers or the Sellers and Buyers]* have been afforded the opportunity and advised to contact a Lawyer, Accountant or *[Canada Revenue Agency Office/Internal Revenue Service **or** your Authorities/Regulators]* or other professionals with any questions/concerns regarding tax liability, exemptions, or the right to apply for any rebates if applicable. The tax and all rules/regulations related to real estate transactions can be complex and it is recommended to the *[Sellers/Buyers or the Sellers and Buyers]* that professional expert advice be obtained prior to entering into this Contract of Purchase and Sale.

28. Taxes | Property Assessments

---

*The Sellers and Buyers accept and acknowledge that *[your Province/your Authorities/Regulators may]* have a system in place for assessment of properties and that the subject property may be reviewed and/or reassessed on an annual basis. The Sellers and Buyers warrant and guarantee that no claims will be made against the Sellers or Buyers' Agents/Representatives/Brokerages for any changes in the property tax as a result of any review or reassessment of the property.

---

29. Taxes | Property Transfer Tax Statement

---

*The Buyers are aware of a _____% Property Transfer Tax up to $_____ of the purchase price and _____% on the balance.
This Schedule is hereby incorporated and forms part of this Contract of Purchase and Sale entered into by the parties as evidenced by their signatures below.

Explanation

These are self-explanatory.

30. Title Insurance

*The Buyers have been advised to research Title Insurance prior to completion of this Contract of Purchase and Sale and it is solely their option whether or not to purchase the same. It is recommended that the Buyers may still want to obtain a Survey and have been advised to research both Title Insurance and Survey information prior to entering into this Contract of Purchase and Sale.

Explanation

This is self-explanatory, and often banks and/or financial institutions will require that buyers obtain Title Insurance. Living in British Columbia, Canada, I personally would always recommend my buyers obtain a survey even if they buy Title Insurance. Title Insurance is very common in the United States.

Title Insurance covers losses incurred if the title's condition is not what was or is registered as with the Land Title Office.

Title Insurance is common in commercial real estate transactions, but it can be valuable to residential transactions as well. Some banks and financial lenders insist on Title Insurance prior to issuing funding.

31. Title Search

*The Buyers have read, acknowledged and accepted the Title Search. In addition to any encumbrances referred to in the preprinted wording in this Contract of Purchase and Sale, the Buyers have read, acknowledge and accept that on Completion/Registration the Buyers will receive title containing:
1. Any non-financial charges, and
2. Any financial charges payable by a utility on its right of way/restrictive covenant/easement or other interest set out in the copy of the Title Search results that are attached, form part of and are incorporated in this Contract of Purchase and Sale and any financial charges payable by a utility on its right of way, restrictive covenant, easement, statutory rights-of-way, building schemes or other interest set out in the copy of the Title Search results. The Buyers are aware that these run with the land and will remain on title.

The Buyers are aware that these charges may affect their use or value of the property and have been advised to seek independent Legal/Professional advice with respect to all charges prior to entering into this Contract of Purchase and Sale.

Do you want to include this?

Charge in Favour Of	*Charge #*
[_____	# _____]
[_____	# _____]
[_____	# _____]

Do you want to include this?
The Sellers warrant and guarantee to provide to the Buyers or the Buyers' Agents/Representatives/ Brokerage *[at no cost to the Buyers]*, within *[3 calendar days]* of acceptance of this Contract of Purchase and Sale by all parties, a full copy/explanation of any and all non-financial legal notations including but not limited to Covenants, Building Schemes, Easements, Restrictive Covenants and any unknown/unclear charges showing on the Title [Surface] Search.

Explanation

Previously, I strongly recommended that the listing agents provide a copy of the Property Disclosure Statement as soon as anyone inquires on the property they have for sale. I also suggested that the agents for the buyers ask for this immediately when inquiring on a property.

I am now urging that the same be done with the Title Search. Both these items were often standard subjects in our Contracts of Purchase and Sale; however, with the disclosure requirements these days, it would be incredibly helpful if everyone could obtain these two documents prior to showing or during the first showing of a property. I have explained why with respect to the Property Disclosure Statement, so now let's discuss why the Title Search is also important.

The Title Search has a wealth of information, and it is a very valuable document. The initial document we receive is called a "Surface Title Search," and it shows if there are any charges registered against the title. It does not explain or provide details of any charges shown. You may have to obtain copies of these specific items in order to explain them to your clients. This can be achieved by ordering documents from a Title Search company, a lawyer/notary or directly from the Land Title Office.

The courts in our area have stated that the onus is on the sellers to know their own title and what has to be cleared from it. That means, to me, that the onus is on both the listing and the buying agents.

The first thing is to check where the title is. It must be in the Land Title Office or you cannot close. Our Title Searches state, "Duplicate Indefeasible Title—None Outstanding," and that is what we want to see. It means the title is in the Land Title Office where it belongs.

If it ever says "Issued to" and a name, then you had better track it down and get it back into the Land Title Office. If it was issued and returned to Land Titles, it will state "Surrendered," so that means it is back in the Land Title Office where it belongs, and the property can transfer to the buyers.

In British Columbia, Canada, if this document is missing or not in the Land Title Office, a closing will not happen. An agent must always make sure it is in the Land Title Office. I always worried and so I personally would send a fax (they won't accept e-mails) confirming in writing that it is in fact in the Land Title Office and we can close.

When the Title Search reveals encumbrances on the title, particularly of a non-financial nature, we have to consider if the buyer needs explicit notification. Technically, private easements must be detailed in the contract, while notification of public easements is optional, as they are covered in the Contract of Purchase and Sale. However, it is recommended that all easements, both public and private, be disclosed.

What is the difference between a public and private easement?

- Public easements are road allowances, sewer easements and hydro right-of-ways. They are easements of governments or Crown corporations.

- Private easements are created by two individuals, and often the other individual is the owner of an adjacent property. This would include things like shared driveways and private roads encroaching on a neighbour's land.

    If on showing a property you notice it shares a driveway, it is important to see that the use is registered on the Title Search. If not, it could just be a friendly agreement, which may not pass with the title.

The key feature of easements and restrictive covenants is that they "run with the land." In other words, just because the property is sold, the status of the easement is not altered. It is still there and still enforceable.

You now must review this "surface search" and see if you need to order any documents giving full explanations of any non-financial charges. This is for the benefit of the sellers and the buyers, so it is the responsibility of the listing agents and buyers' agents to double-check these items. Both agents need to review the Title Search for each of their respective clients.

When I first joined the real estate profession, I ended up making an appointment to visit our Land Title Office in order to understand the entire procedure and what to look for. I personally always look to see what the charges are and really only worry when I see a number—for example, Restrictive Covenant or Easement GB 1234—and nothing else. How could I possibly tell the sellers or buyers what this is? I couldn't. So I would order a copy of it and disclose it using the above statement that could be in most contracts.

When you are writing a Contract of Purchase and Sale, now you can write the sellers' full legal names, their address and the same with the correct legal address and Parcel Identification Number (PID). Take the information from the Title Search. It is amazing how many are wrong on the MLS® printouts. The Title Search is the very best document to use for the sellers' names, address and legal information. Since you have their full names, please take the time to write them in your Contract of Purchase and Sale. Be professional.

You want to see if there is any litigation pending or legal action. You want to see how many mortgages are registered against the title. Do the sellers have enough money to pay everyone, including the real estate agents, from the sale proceeds? These are the main reasons we are asking to receive a copy of the Title Search *prior to* writing a Contract of Purchase and Sale. We want to have time to review all charges and possibly incorporate them in the contract. The bonus is, we now can complete the Contract of Purchase and Sale using the correct information from the Title Search as well.

If I was a buyer and watched you completing the documentation of my offer, I would be impressed. You entered the full legal names of the sellers and their address from the Title Search. You knew if you needed proof of signing authority if it was, for example, a company name, estate sale or Power of Attorney.

You also then ask the buyers for their full legal names; what you are doing is indicating that this is a serious legal document, and you are treating it with professionalism and great care. You are protecting the buyers.

Our preprinted wording in the Contract of Purchase and Sale states that the buyers are accepting charges on the title other than those encumbrances, such as tenancies or private easements. It is advised that you may want to list in the Contract of Purchase and Sale any private easements, restrictive covenants and so on, and be very specific as added protection.

True Story

One agent had this happen to her not so long ago. There was a charge showing GB1234 and no explanation. She did not find out what the charge was, but as we all know, the lawyers/notaries reorder the Title Search just before completion—and of course, the lawyers then order a full detailed copy of the charge. The buyer demanded that it be removed prior to closing.

Now remember, in our jurisdiction, the courts have ruled that it is the sellers' responsibility to know their own title and what has to be cleared from it, but no one bothered to check this unknown numbered charge. It turned out to be an old Canadian Pacific Railway charge that stated that the value of a building to be constructed on the lands must be of a value over $2,000 or words similar to that. So who cares? You cannot build a tree house, play house, or doghouse for under $2,000 these days, but this particular buyer wanted it removed before he closed.

It cost the agent $4,600 and it took over six months to remove it. There goes the commission earned. The lawyers/notaries for the sellers and buyers did undertakings to cover the cost of removing it.

This taught us all a very valuable lesson. If you cannot tell or explain what a charge on the title is, then it is a huge red flag. Do your due diligence. When you write the contract, you could state at whose cost this extra detailed documentation would be if the buyers request further explanation. You should also make notations of any of the restrictive covenants/easements in your contract.

Always do the following:

- Verify the owners' names.

- Confirm the legal description and Property Identification Number.

- Verify the restrictive covenants and easements.

- Always look to see if there is any legal action or litigation pending.

- Check how many mortgages there are. Can the owner clear title, and can the owner pay off all debts? Will you get paid?

- Check where the title is. This can be a serious problem if it has been taken out of the Land Title Office.

  You will find that your job when representing buyers is much easier if you obtain the Surface Title Search upfront and then include the above statement that could be in all your Contracts of Purchase and Sale. This will also benefit the sellers and their agents. Everyone is on the same page and knows how the title will be transferred and what charges will remain on the title.

If it is your listing, give any and all buyers' agents a copy of the Title Search as soon as possible. E-mail it if they call about the property, and it can even be before they view the property. Title Searches are public information. This also makes one less subject in your contracts.

In my opinion, it is the responsibility of both the sellers and the buyers to verify the Title Search. As buyers' agents, you *cannot* say it was the sellers' agents who should have researched and made sure everyone had the proper disclosures. It is amazing how many times I hear agents for the sellers or buyers say, "Well, they wrote the contract/counter-offer, so the problem is theirs." Not so. Everyone must do their due diligence. You cannot put the blame on the other agents just because they wrote the clause or statement, or they forgot to include a protective subject, or you think they should have verified something. It does not work that way, so always triple-check every contract.

Use the 32 statements that could be in most of your Contracts of Purchase and Sale as a checklist for each contract you encounter. It is a great way to make sure nothing is missing and to confirm that you have protected your clients.

Sample Discipline Cases

- A colleague made a number of errors but one of them was that he did not represent his clients' best interests because he did not make sure the buyers knew about a restrictive covenant on the property prior to them removing their subjects. He did not use reasonable efforts to discover any relevant facts, and in this case the restrictive covenant limited the buyers' use of the property and therefore was unsuitable for the buyers' use. Penalty: suspended for approximately three weeks, a fine of $3,000 and completion of educational courses.

An agent and/or brokerage failed:

- to use reasonable efforts to discover relevant facts, in that she failed to discover the nature and full extent of all of the encroachments onto the neighbouring property.

- to advise the buyer that there were no records to independently confirm the permitted status of the carport and driveway encroachments.

- to advise that the buyer should legally find out about the encroachments.

- to use reasonable efforts or any effort at all to discover the restrictive covenant on the title to the property before his clients signed the addendum removing all subjects.

Summary of Title Searches

Arrange to get the Title Search (as well as the Property Disclosure Statement) as soon as a buyer expresses interest in seeing a property. This will give you time to review any and all charges and order copies of any items that may require further investigation.

Disclose any of these items in your Contract of Purchase and Sale, and if the buyers need any further explanation, there is plenty of time for them to verify everything with their lawyers/professional advisors.

If there are more than two mortgages, then you may want to confirm with the listing agents that the sellers will be able to clear title and everyone will be paid. (I have put a sample of a Mortgage Verification document in the appendix, which will allow a listing agent to obtain the current balances on any mortgages with the seller's written authorization.)

32. Waiver of Subjects

* If the Buyers are proceeding with this Contract of Purchase and Sale after having the opportunity to perform their due diligence including the services of Legal/Professional Representatives and the Buyers choose to waive any/all of their subjects instead of fulfilling/removing their beneficial subjects, *[the Buyers hereby warrant and guarantee to execute a waiver at the time of completion. This will be handled by the Lawyers/Notaries at the time of conveyance]*. *[The attached 'Confirm your Advice' is incorporated and forms part of this Contract of Purchase and Sale]*.
This Schedule is hereby incorporated and forms part of this Contract of Purchase and Sale entered into by the parties as evidenced by their signatures below.

Explanation

Sometimes when you are ready to write an offer, the buyers decide that they do not want the industry's standard recommended subjects in their Contract of Purchase and Sale.

They may, as an example, decide they do not want to make a subject to them obtaining insurance for the property. Maybe they have already verified that the property is insurable, or they just don't care about insurance for some personal reason. If this is the case, the smartest advice is to put in the contract that the buyers waived their rights to confirm that there are no pre-existing issues or conditions that would prevent them from obtaining insurance coverage, including but not limited to content, liability and specified perils. This specifically confirms that the buyers chose not to research insurance, and they did not want it to be a protective subject in their Contract of Purchase and Sale.

If they are facing a multiple-offer situation, you will find that the buyers may do all the preliminary research in advance of an offer presentation and waive their right to all subjects. Again, one professional procedure is to waive their rights and quote the specific recommended subjects. This may also be applicable if they do not want one or some of the statements that could be in most of your contracts.

When you are with your buyers and preparing an offer, and they decide to exclude a specific subject or all subjects and/or any statements, then you could have the form with you entitled "Confirm Your Advice" (CYA). This form is really a "Cover Your Ass" document. Whenever you are preparing a contract, have it with you in your file and go through the items relating to the statements and more particularly the subjects. It could also be on your computer if you are working paperless.

If your clients want a statement or subject omitted, then have them *sign* and date beside the item they are omitting, and keep a copy with your documents. (Remember, signatures are much stronger than initials.) You now have proof that you offered them the opportunity to have the industry's standard statements or subjects in the contract, but they chose to waive their inclusion.

This form is also a good checklist to use if you want to review some of the items you should be discussing with your clients. You have included the "Access for All Trades" statement, so if anyone specifically needs to view the property/structures, the sellers have already granted their permission.

CHAPTER 8
SUBJECTS IN MOST CONTRACTS: THE FAMOUS FIVE

Now that we have reviewed the 32 statements that could be in most of your Contracts of Purchase and Sale, let's look at the subjects that are most often in your contracts as well.

When I was teaching a few years ago, my students named the subjects the Famous Five, since there really were only five common subjects that were in almost every offer. These five subjects were and are often included to protect the buyers by giving them time to see if everything is satisfactory, and then they can remove their subjects and proceed to complete the contract.

They then realized that if an agent did not discuss five items with the buyers, that agent had forgotten something. Since that time, the disclosure requirements and changes in our industry have made the common subjects really only three, since two are now statements in most contracts.

The two statements that were subjects back in those days are the Property Disclosure Statement and the Title Search. Now you are asking for both these documents in advance. Also, remember to ask for any other disclosures that may be necessary. We will review these possible disclosures shortly.

This makes the Famous Five now three subjects and two statements. Still, the name Famous Five stuck. If you do not discuss five possible subjects/statements, you will know you have forgotten something. The three subjects are:

1. Financing

    a. Finalization of the Preapproved Mortgage

    b. Satisfactory Financing

    c. Specific Details

    d. Can the Sellers Clear the Title?

2. Insurance

    a. Fire Property Insurance | Residential

    b. Strata Property

3. Inspection

    a. Residential

    b. Strata

and the two statements:

4. Property Disclosure Statement

5. Title Search

In the sections that follow, I will provide the wording you could use for each of the subjects. In that wording:

- *Italics*, [brackets] or <u>underlined</u> portions of the statement indicate that you need to take some form of action prior to using the clause. You may need to add your authorities' regulations or the name of your professional act, or simply revise the statement to suit your needs.

    - [   ] indicates you must fill in information or delete it.

    - [_____] indicates you must fill in information or delete it.

Each statement appears in its own section along with any explanations for using the statement, any information that may help clarify why you may want to include the statement, and a few sample discipline cases if they are applicable to the topic. Occasionally, you will find suggestions relating to the statement.

You can use the detailed information to clarify any concerns with your clients if needed. You want to very simply demonstrate and illustrate why they will be protected by having particular subjects in their contract. It is your job to counsel and advise your clients why these are important protections, and also if they are necessary or not depending on the specific type of property being purchased.

You must possess impeccable skills and establish, if you are a new representative, or re-establish, if you are a seasoned pro, the best comprehensive Contract of Purchase and Sale that will always safely protect your clients and customers. If you employ the methods provided here, you will provide top-notch service to everyone.

The word will soon spread throughout our industry and to real estate buyers and sellers who will begin seeking you out for your assistance and guidance. They will want to work with an agent like you who is known to be trustworthy, determined, precise and cautious, and who genuinely represents clients' interests.

You will notice that I did include the Option Clause, which I have repeated below, for each of the subjects. I have only done this so you can decide if you want to include it or not and also because sometimes a buyer may not want to include all the recommended subjects. By leaving it in, you will remember to consider whether you want to use it. You will also see a * beside it, which indicates that it is already in your statements in most contracts, so you would not have to repeat it with any subjects if you left it in the statement section.

Obviously, you would only insert it once in any Contract of Purchase and Sale. As stated, it is only included repeatedly in case you only selected one subject. It is just for your convenience and is only a reminder should you elect to use it. A full explanation of the reasoning for possibly including the clause is under "Statements" in most contracts.

The Option Clause states:

---

*For good and valuable consideration of [One Dollar $1.00 or $_____] given by the Buyers and hereby acknowledged and received by the Sellers, the Sellers hereby warrant and guarantee that their acceptance of this offer will not be withdrawn or revoked prior to the date for all subjects to be removed.
[Seal]
Time shall remain of the essence.
[Type the word [Seal] exactly as shown].

Now, let's look at the subjects you could use in most of your Contracts of Purchase and Sale.

1a. Financing | Finalization of the Preapproved Mortgage

> This Contract of Purchase and Sale is subject to finalization of the preapproved mortgage *[in the amount of $_____]* on or before *[date]*.
> This subject is for the sole benefit of the Buyers.
> *For good and valuable consideration of *[One Dollar $1.00 or $_____]* given by the Buyers and hereby acknowledged and received by the Sellers, the Sellers hereby warrant and guarantee that their acceptance of this offer will not be withdrawn or revoked prior to the date for all subjects to be removed. [Seal]
> Time shall remain of the essence.
> *[Type the word [Seal] exactly as shown]*.

1b. Financing | Satisfactory Financing

> This Contract of Purchase and Sale is subject to the Buyers obtaining satisfactory financing on or before *[date]*.
> This subject is for the sole benefit of the Buyers.
> *For good and valuable consideration of *[One Dollar $1.00 or $_____]* given by the Buyers and hereby acknowledged and received by the Sellers, the Sellers hereby warrant and guarantee that their acceptance of this offer will not be withdrawn or revoked prior to the date for all subjects to be removed. [Seal]
> Time shall remain of the essence.
> *[Type the word [Seal] exactly as shown]*.

Explanation

Due to the differences in each and every market area, these subjects are only suggestions of what you could include in your Contracts of Purchase and Sale. I think it is important that you understand some of the reasoning behind certain subjects, so I have included further explanations and clarification. I thought it also might help you explain to the public if necessary.

You will notice that when a buyer needs a first mortgage, there really are only three subjects they will choose from. Two of the subjects are "whim and fancy" or "iffy" subjects, because they do not provide specific financing details. The third subject to arranging a mortgage is the subject recommended by most authorities, as it is detailed and very specific.

Is there a problem using "satisfactory" or "preapproved" financing? Some buyers are very savvy and demand that you do not disclose their financing information. They feel that it is no one else's business. This puts you in a dilemma when working with buyers who demand you do what they want whether it is to their benefit or not.

Just remember one thing: Sellers do not have to deal with offers where there is no disclosure of how much financing is needed. They have the sole option of just not responding to this type of offer. They are putting up a very sizeable asset for sale and are entitled to know, so warn your buyers of this. They may not get a counter.

True Story

If I ever had sellers who were willing to accept the "satisfactory" or "preapproved" subjects, I always told them to be aware this was not an offer as such—the buyers could walk at any time—so we would have to wait until the subjects were removed to know if in fact these were genuine buyers.

Some courts have enforced "subject to satisfactory financing" and others have not, so it is a risk and a costly one if it ever went that far. I always made sure that any Contracts of Purchase and Sale with either of those subjects had a very short subject removal time and date, and again I always reinforced with my sellers that we just don't know if they will remove the subjects and purchase the property.

I was always very blunt about this and then gave the sellers the option of accepting these so called "whim and fancy" or "iffy" subjects.

1c. Financing | Specific Details

> This Contract of Purchase and Sale is subject to a new first mortgage being made available to the Buyer by _____, in the amount of $_____ at an interest rate not to exceed _____% per annum calculated half-yearly, not in advance, with a _____-year amortization period, _____- year term and repayable in blended payments of approximately $_____ per month including principal and interest [plus 1/12 of the annual taxes, if required by the mortgagee].
> This subject is for the sole benefit of the Buyers.

Explanation

This subject or something very similar is a recommended subject from most authorities, as it is specific and definitive. It has been upheld in the courts. You must fill in all the blanks for it to be effective.

1d. Financing | Can the Sellers Clear the Title?

This Contract of Purchase and Sale is subject to the Sellers' confirmation and satisfaction with the arrangement of their financial affairs, on or *[date]*, which enable the Sellers to proceed with this sale. This subject is for the sole benefit of the Sellers.

For good and valuable consideration of *[One Dollar $1.00 or $_____]* given by the **Sellers** and hereby acknowledged and received by the **Buyers**, the **Buyers** hereby warrant and guarantee that their acceptance of this offer will not be withdrawn or revoked prior to the date for all subjects to be removed. [Seal]

Time shall remain of the essence.

[Type the word [Seal] exactly as shown].

OR

The Sellers accept and are aware that this property is subject to any/all registered encumbrances and that combined with the obligation for the Sellers to pay commissions and other closing costs, may or do exceed the proceeds of sale from this transaction. This Contract of Purchase and Sale is subject to the Sellers on or before *[date]*, obtaining the written approval of all Charges/Mortgagees and other registered encumbrances as to the final acceptance of this Contract of Purchase and Sale and their agreement to discharge their encumbrances without payment in the aggregate of more than the available proceeds from this transaction.

This subject is for the sole benefit of the Sellers.

For good and valuable consideration of *[One Dollar $1.00 or $_____]* given by the **Sellers** and hereby acknowledged and received by the **Buyers**, the **Buyers** hereby warrant and guarantee that their acceptance of this offer will not be withdrawn or revoked prior to the date for all subjects to be removed. [Seal]

Time shall remain of the essence.

[Type the word [Seal] exactly as shown].

Explanation

There are times when the sellers may not have enough money from the sale proceeds to pay everyone off, and that includes being able to pay you.

Notice that if you use the Option Clause, the wording is reversed, in that it is the sellers asking for the time to make sure they can fulfill this subject and proceed with the contract. The receipt is reversed since the sellers would pay the buyers for the time to arrange subject removal. Be very careful.

The listing agents should have verified the balances of any and all mortgages and confirmed that on completion, the sellers could clear any and all debt and pay the real estate agents. In all honesty, this should have been done when the agent took the listing to sell the property. However, when the buyers review the Title Search and notice a number of mortgages, this would be a red flag, and the agents must confirm with the listing agents that the sellers can in fact deliver the property free and clear of any and all financial encumbrances.

If these agents overlooked verifying balances owing on any financial charges, then this subject should be in the contract to confirm everyone will be able to complete and the title will be delivered free and clear of financial encumbrances. There is a sample form called "Mortgage Verification" that the sellers could sign in order to give their agents permission to obtain any outstanding balances owing. (See appendix.)

True Story

When I began my career in real estate, I did not know to look for the number of mortgages or financial charges showing on title, and therefore I never confirmed that the seller would be able to pay everyone off and pay me.

On my very first listing, I received an offer and everything was great. The buyers' agent asked me for any specific clauses that should be included, so I gave her the City Hall information and tenant's information that I had on my checklist so together we had a great contract. Everything was fine and the subjects got removed, so now I really could celebrate. It was sold.

I had my colleague take a picture of me putting up the sold sticker, and I was in heaven. I was thrilled for my sellers, and actually I was ecstatic for everyone, to be honest.

I remember completing my very first transaction record sheet—don't ever use the word *deal*, it sounds tacky. I had already turned in the contract and transaction record report as required, but now I had to finish it up with subject removal documents. I was on cloud nine. My very first sale.

I can only remember that the commission going to the buyers' brokerage/agent was around $7,000. Documents go to the lawyers/notaries, and now I could count my hard-earned commission.

It was a Friday. The phone rang. It was around 3:00 p.m. I answered and the caller said, "Did you sell the property at [address]?" I said yes. *This was déjà vu.* I felt I had heard these words before.

I had answered with a big smile on my face, since that is what I had been told we should do. Now all of a sudden, my smile was gone. I think I stopped breathing too. My heart was pounding.

It was the buyers' notary who then said that there wasn't enough money to pay off the three mortgages and pay my brokerage and the buyers' brokerage. There was silence, absolute silence. I didn't know what to say. *What do you mean there isn't enough money? What do you mean, three mortgages? This can't be happening.*

I'd already had a disaster with my first buyer, and now I was going to have one with my first seller? My mind was racing. How was I to know there were three mortgages and not enough money for the seller to clear all the debts and pay us?

"This is a joke, right?" I asked. "Someone told you to call me and say this?"

The notary assured me this was for real.

More silence. "Well, what can I do?"

The notary said she couldn't give legal advice, but I did have a very big problem and needed to call her back when I figured it out.

I went to find my managing broker, but he was on a very long lunch break and no one knew if he was coming back. Now what?

I hopped in my car and raced to the seller's house. I did get caught for speeding. Now I owed more money. The policeman said, "Have a nice day."

The seller told me the truth in that yes, he did owe more than we sold the property for, and yes, there wasn't enough money to pay my brokerage and the buyers' brokerage, and he was sorry.

I found out later that it was my responsibility to have checked the Title Search, and if I saw three mortgages I should have found out how much the seller owed. I never even looked at the Title Search, to be very honest. I didn't know to do that. I sure do now. Did I think the Title Search was just a piece of paper given from the sellers to the buyers just because they asked for it?

Well, I wasn't going to let my first sale go the direction of my first purchase. There had to be something I could do. Now was the time to think outside the box. I had $7,055 in my savings account, and believe me, that was all I had to my name. I paid the buyers' brokerage $7,000, their share of the commission, through my brokerage.

I seized all the seller's antiques and had him sign a legal document giving them to me in lieu of commissions. I had $55 left in my savings account. I wondered if that would even cover the cost of advertising the furniture for sale.

I had a lawyer do all the paperwork with me and both brokerages so I didn't go to real estate jail, which is where I was headed. Everything was done in compliance. I think it was. I hope it was.

I sold all the antiques to get my share of the commission and the $7,000 I had paid the buyers' brokerage.

Welcome to your new real estate career, Barb! Isn't this profession wonderful? I always believed that "we sell dirt," and here I was selling furniture privately to get paid. Yes, I did pay tax on this.

After that, Title Searches were added to my list to research and know what I was talking about. I realized just how important it was to be able to read one of these things and know what is going on. I learned everything I could. This was not going to happen again.

Comments

As you see above, there really are only three subjects to the buyers arranging financing or a first mortgage:

1. Finalization of the Preapproved Mortgage

2. Satisfactory Financing

3. Specific Details

    And then there is the "odd" subject:

4. Can the Sellers Clear the Title?

The sellers may have to confirm that they can deliver the title free and clear of any and all financial encumbrances. A professional would research all debt and any other unusual items on the Title Search immediately upon listing the property for sale rather than waiting until there was an offer on the table.

Review these subjects with your buyers, and after you explain them, you would select the appropriate subject they request. You should also review the Option Clause, and after you explain the reasoning behind its possible use, you follow the buyers' instructions.

Remember, you only need to insert the Option Clause once in your contract; it can be with the statements in most of your contracts or under the subjects, but you do not need it more than once.

2a. Fire Property Insurance | Residential

This Contract of Purchase and Sale is subject to the Buyers at their expense confirming that there are no pre-existing issues or conditions that would prevent the Buyers from obtaining insurance coverage including but not limited to content, liability, specified perils on or before *[date]*. This subject is for the sole benefit of the Buyer.

The Sellers agree to allow access for any of these parties if required including those already agreed to in the Access for All Trades Statement.

Do you want to include this?

[The Sellers warrant and guarantee to give a copy of their current Insurance Policy to the Buyers or the Buyers' Agents/Representatives/Brokerage within [3] calendar days of acceptance of this Contract of Purchase and Sale by all parties and at no cost to the Buyers.]

The Buyers have been advised to seek independent Legal/Insurance/Professional advice.

*For good and valuable consideration of [One Dollar $1.00 or $_____] given by the Buyers and hereby acknowledged and received by the Sellers, the Sellers hereby warrant and guarantee that their acceptance of this offer will not be withdrawn or revoked prior to the date for all subjects to be removed. [Seal]

Time shall remain of the essence.

[Type the word [Seal] exactly as shown].

2b. Insurance | Strata Property

Summary of Coverage of Insurance and [*Condominium Homeowner, Landlord or Tenants Insurance Policy]

This Contract of Purchase and Sale is subject to the Buyers receiving and approving at no cost to the Sellers, a copy of the Insurance Policy and/or 'Summary of Coverage of Insurance' for the Owners of Strata Plan *[Name/Number]* and subject to the Buyers confirming the availability of insurance coverage including content, liability, specified perils *[and_____]* on or before *[date]*.

AND/OR [I personally would include both these subjects.]

This Contract of Purchase and Sale is subject to the Buyers confirming that there are no pre-existing issues or conditions that would prevent the buyers from obtaining insurance coverage including content, liability, specified perils *[and_____]* on or before *[date]*.

This condition is for the sole benefit of the Buyer.

Do you want to include this?

[The Sellers warrant and guarantee to give a copy of their current Insurance Policy to the Buyers or the Buyers' Agents/Representatives/Brokerage within [3] calendar days of acceptance of this Contract of Purchase and Sale by all parties and at no cost to the Buyers.]

The Buyers have been advised to seek independent Legal/Insurance/Professional advice.

The Sellers agree to allow access for any of these parties if required including those already agreed to in the Access for All Trades Statement.

*For good and valuable consideration of [One Dollar $1.00 or $_____] given by the Buyers and hereby acknowledged and received by the Sellers, the Sellers hereby warrant and guarantee that their acceptance of this offer will not be withdrawn or revoked prior to the date for all subjects to be removed. [Seal]

Time shall remain of the essence.

[Type the word [Seal] exactly as shown].

Explanation

Do you think "satisfactory insurance" is a "whim and fancy" clause or an "iffy" clause? The above sample insurance clauses are detailed and specific. As explained with the financing information, the "subject to satisfactory insurance" that some agents are using may not be specific or definitive enough. I often see agents failing to make the obtaining of insurance a subject at all. Be careful. Insurance can and has been denied due to hazards like forest fires, grow-ops and meth-lab problems.

3a. Inspection of the Property | Residential

This Contract of Purchase and Sale is subject to the Buyers, on or before [date], at the Buyers' expense, obtaining and approving an inspection report [or professional inspection] against any defects [whose cumulative cost of repair exceeds $_____ and] which reasonably may adversely affect the property's use or value.
This subject is for the sole benefit of the Buyers.
The Sellers agree to allow access for any of these parties if required including those already agreed to in the Access for All Trades Statement.
*For good and valuable consideration of [One Dollar $1.00 or $_____] given by the Buyers and hereby acknowledged and received by the Sellers, the Sellers hereby warrant and guarantee that their acceptance of this offer will not be withdrawn or revoked prior to the date for all subjects to be removed. [Seal]
Time shall remain of the essence.
[Type the word [Seal] exactly as shown.]

[Remember you cannot give out copies of the Report without written consent of the Inspector and/or Buyers/Sellers.]

Don't forget the oil tank/septic statement/subject. If your buyers ever waived the right to an inspection remember to add in about an oil tank or septic tank. It is very important. We have seen so many problems with these items.

3b. Inspections of the Property | Strata

This Contract of Purchase and Sale is subject to the Buyers, on or before *[date]*, at the Buyers' expense, obtaining and approving an inspection report *[or professional inspection]* against any defects *[whose cumulative cost of repair exceeds $_____ and]* which reasonably may adversely affect the property's use or value.
The Sellers agree to allow access for any of these parties if required including those already agreed to in the Access for All Trades Statement.
This subject is for the sole benefit of the Buyers.

The Sellers/Sellers' Agents/Representatives/Brokerage warrant and guarantee to arrange, on reasonable notice, for the purposes of inspection, access to the suite and common areas such as, but not limited to, the roof, the electrical room, boiler or furnace room, parking areas, storage areas and recreational areas, at no cost to the Buyers/Buyers' Agents/Representatives/Brokerage.
*For good and valuable consideration of *[One Dollar $1.00 or $_____] *given by the Buyers and hereby acknowledged and received by the Sellers, the Sellers hereby warrant and guarantee that their acceptance of this offer will not be withdrawn or revoked prior to the date for all subjects to be removed. [Seal]
Time shall remain of the essence.
[Type the word [Seal] exactly as shown.]

[Remember you cannot give out copies of the Report without written consent of the Inspector and/or Buyers/Sellers.]

Explanation

The last of the subjects is subject to an inspection or a professional inspection, and it is your responsibility to advise the buyers to have one. You have an obligation to recommend that everyone obtain a (professional) inspection on a property. It is part of your duties, so make sure if the buyers ever refuse to do an inspection or a professional inspection that you have written documentation that they waived their rights to do so. You could also use the "Confirm Your Advice" form and have them sign and date this exclusion. The onus is always on you to prove that you did your due diligence and fulfilled your duties. This also applies to recommending legal/professional or any other specific advice to all parties. The onus is again on you.

If the buyers do waive their right to a professional inspection, please make sure you have proof that there is no oil tank. Get the documentation to prove it was removed or decommissioned or whatever, and this again applies to any other items specific to your area. You must never waive the right to an oil-tank inspection; it is just too dangerous and can be very costly, especially if there was contamination. Again, the onus is on you.

There certainly are a lot of items we may have to prove, aren't there? Oh well, just do it right and you will have no problems. We have to comply. That's our law.

Warning Regarding Distributing the Inspection Report

Some sellers want the following statement in their contract:

In the event the Buyers do not remove their "Subject to Inspection" of the property or find the report unsatisfactory, the Buyers agree to give a copy of the report to the Sellers including [if applicable] any estimates they have.

Do you have written permission from the inspection company/inspector and/or the sellers/buyers or others to distribute and/or provide these copies?

Also, some sellers are having a preinspection report done to give out to prospective buyers; again, do they have written permission from the inspection company/inspector?

Remember, you cannot give out copies of the inspection report without written consent of the inspector and/or buyers/sellers. See the "Permission to Distribute the Inspection Report" form in the appendix.

CHAPTER 9
THE ORDER OF MY CONTRACTS

Now that we've gone through all 32 statements and the Famous Five, you can see that some are just common sense and others are just for you to consider, but remember that the onus is on you to prove that you protected the public, so let's protect them.

If your clients have any concerns, no matter how small, it is critical that you make the statements into subjects. You might as well know in advance how they feel about the written contract, and it is a red flag for you if they are concerned about anything. Find out in advance.

You can change the order to suit you, but always do it the same way so you never forget anything. It is important that you make this a habit. Put any required disclosures on top of your authority's Contract of Purchase and Sale for signatures prior to viewing the Contract of Purchase and Sale. The actual requirement for most disclosures is that they must be signed and dated prior to entering into a contract.

Train yourself to:

- Use the checklist *prior to* writing an offer. (See appendix.)

- Use the second checklist when the buyers are *ready to* write an offer. (See appendix.)

- Use the Contract of Purchase and Sale from your authorities.

- Review the 32 statements and select the ones that could be in most of your contracts.

- Review and select subjects from the Famous Five.

- Review the property specifics (these are the particular items that relate specifically and only to the property your buyers are making an offer on; see next chapter).

I always do things in the same order for my contracts: statements first, then subjects, then property specifics. Always pretend it is you or your family buying. And remember: You *must* always cross-reference receipt of separate documents, handwritten or otherwise.

The onus and burden of proof is on you to show how you run your professional business. Stick to the plan and blueprint I am giving you. Follow the rules and always write your Contracts of Purchase and Sale in the same order every time. You are less likely to make any mistakes, less likely to forget anything and if ever needed your authorities will be able to review your previous contracts and know that you do have a consistent method to help protect the public. You do review everything with them giving them the opportunity to seek independent legal/professional advice if needed or even if they just wanted to do so or maybe you recommend that they do so. You also are allowing them to make their own informed decisions but only after considering each and every detail. You always explain the benefits and the risks of every step of the purchase and sale. You sincerely do care about them and their real estate transaction and will do everything in your power to educate and protect them.

CHAPTER 10
PROPERTY SPECIFICS

We have reviewed the 32 statements that could be in most Contracts of Purchase and Sale and the subjects—the Famous Five—that are most commonly used in a contract. You are sitting with your buyers, and now you have to think of the items that are applicable to this particular property. These are what I refer to as the "property specifics."

You want to jot down what needs to be written into the contract to protect your buyers—and remember, real estate must be in writing, so you do not want to forget anything at this point. If you have adapted to my unique checklists for preparing a contract, the odds of you forgetting anything are minimal. It would be awful if now, approaching the end of the contract, you forgot or missed an item specific to your buyer's purchase.

For the purposes of this section, I will present some examples that could be found to be applicable and show you how to put them into the contract following the statements and subjects. You should keep all your contracts in the same order every single time to help make sure you never forget anything. Be consistent.

When you made the original appointment to view the property with your buyers, you asked for the Property Disclosure Statement and Title Search, and you've reviewed these and included them in the previous statement section of the contract. Now you have to think, *What else would I need to put in if I or my family was buying this property? What is specific and needs written confirmation so the parties are all on the same page and there will never be any misunderstandings?*

The property specifics are the particular items that relate specifically and only to the property your buyers are making an offer on. Remember, you are pretending it is you or your family buying. You will be amazed at what you think of that needs to be in the contract, including the statements and subjects.

I am sharing all this with you so that you will never forget anything. For example, you will always remember to cross-reference receipt of separate disclosures, you will always include allowing for access by any of the trades, and you will be reminded to disclose your remuneration and/or any referral fees. All these statements and subjects put you in the forefront of writing an enforceable Contract of Purchase and Sale. You are as close to a 10 out of 10 as possible.

Let's assume that this property has the following concerns for you to explain to your buyers and obtain their lawful instructions on including and/or excluding written verification of them. These examples are just selected at random to give you an idea of what you could put in the property specifics included in a contract.

- The buyers want to pay more than the asking price to ensure acceptance of their offer. They absolutely fell in love with this home and want it.

- The buyers also mention that they really would like to have a second visit of the property prior to closing date.

- The listing agents have told you that you cannot present your own offer and that you must e-mail or fax your offer to their office.

- The listing agents have also said that they cannot present your offer today and have been instructed by their sellers not to present any offers until Sunday night at 7:00 p.m.

- This is a single-family home with an unauthorized (illegal) basement suite. The basement suite is not tenant-occupied, although sometimes you may have to consider the possibility of tenancy information being reviewed.

Let's take a look at how you would handle these concerns, either by adding language to the contract or keeping your clients informed.

Over Asking Price

Add the following statement to the contract:

> The Buyers are aware that the amount of this offer to purchase is in excess of the listing price or advertised price for this property and waive any rights to subsequent recovery of such higher amount.

Right of Reinspection/Viewing

Add the following statement to the contract:

> The Sellers and Buyers mutually agree that the Sellers shall have the right to reinspect/view the land/property/buildings/structures *[one/two]* further times at a mutually agreed upon time provided that *[24 hour]* *[written]* notice is given from the Buyers to the Sellers. The maximum time the Buyers are allowed for the agreed visits is *[2 hours]*. The Buyers at the time of serving the written notice will specifically specify who will accompany them on the visits including but not limited to the Buyers/Buyers' Agents/Representatives/Brokerage/Architects/Interior Designers/ Contractors and the like Professions for pre-measuring/decorating/planning purposes. The Sellers warrant that this notice will not be unreasonably withheld.
> The Sellers agree to allow access for any of these parties if required including those already agreed to in the Access for All Trades Statement.

Presentation of Offers

Your buyers are entitled to know that the sellers have given written instructions regarding delaying any showings or presentation times. They would also have written instructions if you are not allowed to present your buyers' offer. (See the forms "Presentation of Offers | Delayed to a Specific Date and/or Time" and "Presentation of Offers | Direction That Only the Listing Agents to Present Offers" in the appendix.)

A prudent and professional listing agent would send you these two written authorizations/ instructions at the time you initially inquired on the property. These would be sent along with the Property Disclosure Statement and the Title Search. This would also be the time for the listing agent to send any other mandatory disclosures, including disclosure of material latent defects, disclosure if the agent or a family member had an interest in the property, proof of signing authority if the contract is not being signed by the sellers or if the sellers are a business or corporation, etc.

These types of notations should also be in the REALTOR® remarks in the MLS® listing. In British Columbia, Canada, we are also required to include these notations on Schedule A of the listing contract.

Often a listing agent will make notations regarding documentation you may need prior to writing an offer in the REALTOR® remarks so you can ask for and obtain everything upfront. Also, with our improved co-operation with each other, many listing agents automatically e-mail all documentation/disclosures/instructions to any buyer's agents who call on the property. It doesn't matter if the buyers have even viewed the property; they just make sure any information an agent may need is delivered promptly. This is a perfect solution, and I hope everyone will begin doing it if they aren't already.

This is just an automatic procedure they have in place, and it makes everyone's job so much easier and more efficient. Not only that, there will be far fewer changes to the original offer and fewer counter-offers because the buyers have the sellers' wishes upfront and prior to writing their Contract of Purchase and Sale.

True Story

I had listed a triplex for sale, and since I couldn't have open houses by myself with three suites, we agreed to showings on Thursday evenings from 6:00 p.m. until 7:00 p.m. and Saturdays from noon until 1:00 p.m. Today you would put this in your REALTOR® remarks and also add it to your Schedule in the listing agreement. Remember, you are actually delaying the showing times to Thursdays and Saturdays, so when a colleague calls you about viewing the property, you would send them these written instructions signed by the sellers. (See the form "Presentation of Offers | Delayed to a Specific Date and/or Time" and the form "Presentation of Offers | Direction That Only the Listing Agents to Present Offers" in the appendix.) Also send the Property Disclosure, Title Search and any other disclosures required.

After I finally realized what our industry was all about, I often had a typewritten list of what was important to the sellers, including their preferred completion and possession dates. (We did not have the luxury of computers back then.) I listed any appliances not included— anything and everything that might help make a buyer's offer to my sellers cleaner. I had to fax it to them in those days, but it was worth it to help my colleagues, clients and myself.

This saved a lot of handwritten counter-clauses and statements and often there were fewer subjects. There was a good chance the offer could come together much more easily since dates were often what my sellers needed. Price is not always the only concern; terms do matter as well.

With the information superhighway today, you can do this much quicker and easier than I ever could, so why don't you just do it? It will benefit you and your sellers as well. Give the buyers everything they need to prepare an offer that incorporates the sellers' wants and needs, and you are more than halfway there.

Disclosures will be acknowledged and cross-referenced in the contract, so that means fewer subjects. Dates may be able to dovetail and coordinate with everyone. Appliances included are acceptable to all, so nothing has to be crossed off creating a counter-offer. It's a perfect way to do business, and the public will be impressed.

Ideally, both agents co-operate and work together to prepare an initial offer as close to everyone's wants and needs as possible. Now you can work as a team toward a satisfactory sale. It is a win-win for everyone.

Suggestion: In the appendix, there is a form entitled "Notice to Tenants for Multiple Showings." I also included a sample "Notice to Tenants" for a one-time showing. I only included these for your convenience, since this really is applicable to the listing agents. In our area, it is important to always state the reason for any showings, so I have pretyped it on the forms for you.

Unauthorized Accommodation

Add the following statement to the contract:

> 1. The Buyer is aware that the property contains unauthorized accommodation and has been informed of the consequences of such ownership and the potential loss of income should the rental use be discontinued.
>
> 2. The Buyers acknowledge having received separate written disclosure of a material latent defect relating to unauthorized accommodation/illegal suites prior to the signing of this Contract and have been advised to seek independent Legal/Professional advice prior to entering into this Contract of Purchase and Sale.
>
> 3. *The Sellers warrant and guarantee there are no outstanding Work, Fire, Safety, Health or Environmental orders with any *[City/Municipal/Provincial/Governmental/ Environmental]* Authorities/Regulators *[including the Strata Council, Strata Corporation and Property Management Companies if applicable]*.
>
> *Is this already included in your Statements pages?*
> *Any and all documentation provided by the Sellers to the Buyers or the Buyers to the Sellers will be attached to, incorporated and form part of this Contract of Purchase and Sale.

The above covers the acknowledgement of the unauthorized accommodation and that, should any governmental authorities shut it down, the buyers could lose any income. This should be acknowledged in every contract, even if the suite is vacant and/or your buyers tell you they are not going to rent it out. Put this statement in your Contract of Purchase and Sale.

It also acknowledges that the buyers received separate written disclosure of the material latent defect prior to entering into the contract.

Using the Material Latent Defect Form

If for some reason you did not receive written disclosure prior to presentation of your offer, or the sellers did not make this disclosure on the Property Disclosure Statement, you could use the form "Material Latent Defects | Disclosure," found in the appendix, or handwrite the disclosure on a piece of paper.

Because you are not allowed to present your own offer, you would ask the listing agent to have the disclosure signed *prior* to entering into the contract, and then it is done. Your buyers would have signed the form in advance. You knew from viewing the property and your research that the suite was unauthorized, and that makes it a material latent defect (lack of permits).

The "Material Latent Defects" form could be filled in and completed by your buyers if you cannot get the required disclosure in advance from the listing agents/sellers. What you would do is have the buyers sign it, put it on top of your Contract of Purchase and Sale, and have the sellers sign it prior to viewing the contract to be on the safe side. It must be signed prior to entering into a contract. This would work. Your buyers have already signed the disclosure.

If you read or when touring the property you notice there is an unauthorized accommodation, renovations without permits or other possible material latent defects, then you could go with this format, although it would just be so easy and fantastic if the listing agents would send it to you the day you initially phone and inquire about the property.

Whenever there is unauthorized accommodation or renovations without permits and the like, do not forget to do your due diligence by confirming the status with your governmental agencies. If possible, confirm the advice you received from all authorities in writing (fax) so you have a paper trail. Your buyers should also make their own separate inquiries.

You have cross-referenced receipt of this disclosure in your Contract of Purchase and Sale under #2 above in the Unauthorized Accommodation statement. Remember, too, it is important to cross-reference acknowledgement of any other separate disclosures, written pieces of paper, or whatever. You must never forget to put this in your contract.

The "Material Latent Defects | Disclosure" form states the following:

❐ The "Property" as legally described above **HAS** the following Material Latent Defects.
The property contains an unauthorized suite.

❐ To the best of the Sellers' knowledge, the Sellers warrant and guarantee that there are <u>NO FURTHER</u> material latent defects other than those disclosed above.

☐ To the best of the Sellers' knowledge, the Sellers warrant and guarantee that there are <u>NO</u> material latent defects.

Your buyers would have filled in the first statement shown above, checked off or initialled the second statement, and signed and dated their acknowledgement at the bottom of the disclosure form. Now, once the sellers sign and date it, everyone will be in compliance. How easy is that?

Sample Discipline Cases

- An agent did not confirm that the property was unauthorized or non-conforming. He knew or ought to have known that the legality of the suite was important to the buyers. Penalty: suspended for approximately one week, a fine of $1,000 and completion of remedial education courses.

- An agent advertised in the REALTOR® remarks that the suites were legal when in fact they were not. Penalty: suspended for approximately one week, a fine of $1,000 and completion of remedial education courses.

- An agent failed to use reasonable care and skill, in that he advertised the property on MLS® as having two legal suites without having first obtained confirmation from the city that the suites complied with all applicable legal requirements.

- An agent failed to disclose to the buyers that the necessary building permits and approvals were not obtained.

When there is unauthorized accommodation in any property, it is your obligation to verify everything with your governmental authorities. Do your due diligence and act with care and skill.

There are always three statements that would be written into your Contract of Purchase and Sale whenever there is an unauthorized accommodation, whether an unapproved/illegal suite, an opened-up loft area in a condominium or an enclosed garage with further living space. Do not relax your duties even if your buyers say they are never going to rent out a space. You must always disclose it is unauthorized and the authorities could close it down.

True Story

I had sold the buyers a triplex—unauthorized, of course, but I thought I knew my property specifics and was pretty much an expert by this time. Well, there was one thing I didn't cover, and I will never ever forget it now.

The unauthorized triplex completed right on time and everything was fantastic. I had even been paid this time. This was a good thing.

Then on Friday around 3:00 p.m. (sound familiar?), the phone rang and the buyer was screaming in my ear. I don't mean yelling, I mean *screaming*. We had become great acquaintances, so what had happened? He had even sent me a reference testimonial.

I was also the listing agent on this property and had advertised the unauthorized accommodation in the REALTOR® remarks and in newspaper ads. I used the recommended wording.

I also had the sellers sign their consent that I could advertise their unauthorized accommodation. (See appendix form "Unauthorized Accommodations/Renovations | Consent to Advertise.")

I asked the buyer to calm down and talk to me. Take a deep breath. He did, and then he told me that they had received a letter from the city to close the unauthorized basement suite.

I was absolutely at a loss for words. The city knows of zillions of unauthorized/illegal suites, but even back then they didn't go looking to shut them down; they only acted on a complaint. I listened carefully to the buyer and said how sorry I was, but it wasn't me who called the city. He did not believe me. He was angry and threatening to ruin my name, sue me and heaven knows what else. He ranted and raved for a good 20 minutes or more.

My father taught me a trick: If someone is screaming at you on the phone, wait until *you personally* are in the middle of a sentence and hang up. The caller will truly think they were disconnected, because who in their right mind would hang up in the middle of their own comments?

I decided against using this tactic and let the buyer carry on for another 5 or 10 minutes. I apologized and said I would see what I could find out.

When something like this happens, you cannot just leave it. Remember, I said there is always a sense of urgency in our profession; well, this is one of those times to deal with the problem immediately. I didn't want this buyer badmouthing me all over town, but I didn't know if I could get through to the city since it was now after 4:00 p.m. No luck, they were closed.

I know that there are two main reasons the city tries to close a suite. One is that they receive a complaint from the public, and it is usually that the tenants are hogging all the street parking and the owners in the area cannot park in front of their own home. The second is that the tenants put the garbage out on Monday and pickup is not until Friday. The garbage cans are overflowing, and often animals and birds get into the can and garbage is up and down the lane, in garden areas of the neighbours, and there is a big mess everywhere. Those are the two most common complaints.

In our area, a person must file the complaint in writing. I would never report anyone about this, even my worst enemy. Also, the city will never disclose the name of the complainant.

I went home and grabbed a few beers, sat down and pretended this was happening to me. (Oh, it *was* happening to me!)

How could I prove to the buyer that I did not report his unauthorized suite? I had two days to figure this out. I would never do anything to cause the closing of the suite. He was probably drinking beer too and getting madder by the minute, because I did receive a few more pages to call him. Two of those pages were in the middle of the night. This was not going well at all.

Monday morning, I made numerous calls to the city, but they just stuck by their rules: "We will never release the name of the complainant." I was trying to prove that I did not report the unit to the city, and more importantly, I also wanted to see what had happened and maybe I could help him out of this mess. Maybe there was something else we could do so that the city didn't actually close the suite or stop the usage of the unit.

The only other idea I had was, could I convince the city to confirm that I was *not* the complainant? Would that work? I decided that this was the only option. I had to help my buyer from closing the suite no matter what. I had not done anything wrong, but I owed him the professional courtesy of at least trying to prevent him losing income.

After the calls on Monday, I typed a letter to the buyer confirming that yes, in fact, the city had received a complaint but guaranteeing that it was not from Barbara Bell-Olsen and/ or my brokerage. I knew this was the only thing that would save me.

I missed the Monday office tour of new listings, ran to my car, put it in drive, and drove into the cement wall. I should have put it in reverse. Hello? Okay, calm down, Barb, and don't get a speeding ticket. I didn't.

I parked and from my glove box filled the parking meter to the maximum. Always carry rolls of change in your vehicle for parking meters or other special needs.

Off I went, pretending I was professional and calm, but inside I was shaking like you cannot imagine. I got my number and waited and waited for my turn at the counter.

Finally I was called to the counter and explained my situation.

The woman just laughed and said, "You have to be kidding me." I told her I wasn't and how serious this was. I asked to see her supervisor. By now I was close to tears. This would not be the time to cry. I needed to keep it together.

The counter assistant popped her head into the supervisor's office and was chuckling the whole time as she explained what I wanted and showed him my letter. It was typed on a plain 8½ x 11 piece of paper.

He cracked up too, but then he looked up and saw my eyes. I think that gave it away. I learned then it was time to buy waterproof mascara. I removed my name badge. It was time to be a secret agent around the public in the waiting room, especially if I was going to fall apart.

He sauntered on over and I thought, *Well, this is my last chance*. There was a pen in my hand and it was vibrating, which he noticed as well. Yes, I looked professional, tears in my eyes, black mascara running down my face and that darn pen doing a dance all by itself. Definitely professional!

I literally had to yank the pen out of my hand, and no, I didn't throw it. I just laid it on the counter where it rolled off the other side.

I recognized him when he got to the counter. He was the gentleman I spent almost three hours with learning the rules about unauthorized accommodation after an earlier problem. I had also talked to him numerous times doing my research to be a so-called expert.

He was the gruff voice on the other end of the phone at 3:05 p.m. on subject removal day who asked if I had sold the property with "stop work orders" and "no occupancy." Oh great. It was Clancy.

Not only that, it was Monday. The rules say when you want help or a bank loan or anything like that, never do it on a Monday. Wait until Friday when everyone is happy and excited with the weekend coming.

"Good morning, Clancy."

"Good morning, Barb." He knew my name, or else he read it in my letter. I prefer to think he knew my name, but I sure hoped he wasn't remembering me in a bad light.

He then said, "Barb, you really did it this time, didn't you?"

I swore to him I didn't report the suite and how upset I was that the buyer really thought I did. He went on the computer, but he already knew I didn't do it or I wouldn't be at his office.

"This is a pretty ingenious idea you have," he says. "You know we can't say who reported the property, don't you?"

"Yes, I do," I said rather meekly, "but I really need your help, and this was the only thing I could come up with. Look, Clancy, I even typed it on blank paper so you could just photocopy it onto your letterhead." I looked up at him and thought he had a hint of a small smile, but it quickly vanished. Was it my imagination?

I also told him that we needed to discuss the closing down of the suite, and maybe he could help me with that too. I didn't want to push it too much at this point.

He told me to go wait in the seating area, and he turned his back on me and was gone. I waited for what seemed like an eternity and had to go to the washroom, but I wasn't leaving until I knew if I could convince him to help me and my buyer. I could not let their suite be shut down. Legs crossed and foot swinging, I sat there in the hardest chair ever. I think I was stuck to the chair.

Finally, he came back and called me up. I thought, *Okay, Barb, this is it, you have to plead your case*, but as I opened my mouth he told me to hush and said, "Here." He gave me an official letter that said exactly what I had typed, that I did not report the suite but they could not reveal who actually did. I was shocked and looked up. This gruff man was smiling, and I mean really smiling. Who says *hush* these days?

I couldn't even begin to thank him, but he told me to hush again and said, "Barb, you spent hours in here learning what you needed to know for your profession, and as you called it 'protecting everyone,' and then you called me a bunch of times making sure you really understood what was involved. You were so persistent, and you obviously care about the rules and what to do. Now you arrive with this brilliant idea, right off the wall, of how we could help prove your innocence. I decided to approve your letter and help you out of this mess. I hope it works."

I couldn't say a word; I didn't even know what to say. How could this be happening? He was saving my career, my life, and everything that mattered to me. I couldn't believe it.

He then told me on the quiet that the reporting of the unauthorized accommodation could be handled a different way, and the suite would not have to be closed. He said the complaint was a minor infraction, and they would help the buyer work through the problems. Again, I could not believe how much he was willing to help me and my buyer. He kept his word. The suite was not shut down.

To this day, I still can't believe it. Thank you so much, Clancy.

I turned to run to the washroom, and he called me back to say that he had already sent the letter to the buyer, and he had phoned and left a message that it was definitely not me who reported them and that they did not have to close the suite.

I was standing there with my legs crossed as he said, "Good luck, Barb. I really hope it works. It was a brilliant idea you had." He said *brilliant!* Wow, did I ever feel great. I had solved both problems by thinking outside the box. I was so relieved, but I couldn't stand there any longer. I had to go, *in more ways than one!*

He then handed me some information about advertising unauthorized/illegal accommodations and told me to call him once I had reviewed it, as he was sure I would have some questions.

It was Monday. This was the man who shut down my first buyer sale; this was the man who spent hours teaching me what I needed to know about the legalities of a building, and now he saved my life and my buyer's life. What an incredible man!

I bolted to the washroom and of course there was a line, but I made it.

I headed to my car. The parking lady was beginning to write me a ticket, but I talked myself out of that one—I think it was just because I was babbling on about how great Clancy was. You couldn't have shut me up at that point. It was amazing. It was wonderful. The buyer did apologize; he made some small changes to bring the suite up to code, and everything was fine.

When you have problems, face them head-on with a sense of urgency, and definitely think outside the box.

Advertising of Unauthorized/Illegal Suites

Today, when you list an unauthorized suite, you must disclose it in the REALTOR® remarks so your colleagues know, and on your Schedule to the listing agreement.

A number of agents are now putting this in the MLS® public remarks because it would be an easy way to acknowledge any material latent defects. If it was in the public remarks, the buyers could just sign (initial) and date acknowledgement of the disclosure, which would be prior to entering into a Contract of Purchase and Sale, thereby meeting the disclosure requirements in our market area.

After my experience with the triplex with an unauthorized suite, and due to the fact that since that time I have always had my sellers sign a "Consent to Advertise Our Unauthorized Accommodations/Renovations" form (see appendix), I would worry if this was in the public remarks. There are a number of people who look for this type of accommodation in the MLS® printouts and in any advertising, and they might very well report it to the city, which always has to act on a written complaint. I think you could be leaving yourself wide open for possible litigation, but this is just my personal opinion. I think you should advise your sellers of the possible ramifications and let them make their own informed decision after signing the above form or something similar.

We have a duty to warn our buyers of purchasing these types of accommodation that could in fact be shut down or the rental use discontinued, and we do this in writing. Remember, if an unauthorized/illegal suite is vacant or if your buyers tell you they are not going to rent it out, you must still make the appropriate disclosures. Be sure to cross-reference that disclosure was received in the contract and include the statement that the buyers are aware that the accommodation could be shut down. (See the section on unauthorized accommodations earlier in this chapter.)

CHAPTER 11
TENANCIES AND TRUE STORIES

Be very careful with respect to tenanted properties. Sometimes the sellers will tell you that the son is staying in the basement unit, or as in the two true stories below, a nanny was an employee allowed to use the suite or a sister staying in the basement suite was moving to England with her sister the owner, who lived in the upper floor of the house. Do not assume these people are not tenants. You must treat them as if they were.

My Very First Buyer

I've mentioned a few times that my first experience with a buyer was something of a disaster. Here's the true story.

The phone rang, and it was an acquaintance of mine. I had followed up with him and kept in touch, and he told me he wanted to buy a particular property that was still under construction and had four suites. No problem. I knew exactly what to do.

I made the appointment. We went to view the property with the listing agent, and my acquaintance wanted to buy it. *Wow, this is easy.* Now what? I had never written an offer in my life, much less on four suites that we were told were legal, two of which were still under construction. Hey, I could do this.

I found my managing broker, but he had to go home. It was 5:03 p.m., so he just said, "Good luck, Barb." Seems to me I had heard those words before on the day I started. So he left, and I found the form with all the carbon paper and thought, *Well, now what?*

I phoned my buyer, and we decided that during the subject to satisfactory financing, he could do any research needed regarding the city/governmental information—but remember, the listing agent told us all four suites were legal, so my buyer wasn't too worried.

I had no idea, so I wrote the Contract of Purchase and Sale stating only one subject: "Subject to satisfactory financing on or before" and allowed 10 days. "This subject is for the sole benefit of the Buyer." I knew he wanted interest on his $5,000 deposit, so I phoned him back and got his Social Insurance Number and plastered that on the front page of the contract too. Both of these methods were totally off the wall, and I could have been in real estate jail for even thinking I could get away with this. I didn't get caught that time. I did, though, make a point of learning from it.

I handwrote the contract, hopped in my car and raced to his house. I didn't get a ticket for speeding either. I had luck on my side and things were going along smoothly. I got there, and he signed the contract and gave me a personal cheque for $5,000 since I said on acceptance, not on subject removal.

Suggestion: If you are taking a deposit upon acceptance, you want to state: "Deposit to be $_____ by way of bank draft, money order *[or bank wire transfer] upon acceptance of this Contract by all parties." This clarifies that the deposit is due once the sellers and buyers come to a mutual agreement. [See sections 8 and 9 on deposits in chapter 7.]

In the end, what happened was that the sellers accepted our offer, the personal cheque was in my Brokerage Trust Account, and I noticed I used the wrong contract form but, oh well, what the heck. No one else mentioned it. Not only that, I didn't press hard enough for the subject and Social Insurance Number and closing dates to go through, so I had to get the original back and make photocopies for everyone.

I never addressed the tenancy issues in the top-floor suites at all, and I made completion, possession and adjustment all the same date. I should have at least specified that possession was a specific time after the sellers had been paid and the property had been registered in the buyer's name.

I didn't even include any appliances, except I did say "as per the MLS® listing." What was I thinking? That is really clear and definitive, isn't it? This was my very first brilliant contract. Talk about being lazy and writing a sloppy contract. This whole thing was totally out of my realm of expertise—which was, when I think of it, nothing. I had no concept of what I was doing, and I should have obtained help from an experienced colleague.

Now it was subject removal day, and I was all excited, my very first sale—and remember, I didn't do any follow-up with my buyer, including checking at City Hall, finding out about the tenants or the new construction. I had no idea I was supposed to do this, so I didn't.

On Friday, 3:05 p.m., the subject removal date, the phone rings. I answer and this gruff, powerful, and very loud voice says, "Did you sell the property at [address]?"

I said yes.

The man, whose name I found out was Clancy (remember him from the story in the previous chapter), said, "If you do sell it to your buyer, we the city will be shutting it down immediately."

My heart sank, my mind went blank and my hands were shaking. I think my pen flew across the room like a dart. "Pardon me?"

He said the city had already posted Stop Work Orders on the two lower suites under construction and No Occupancy Permits.

He then asked me if I had seen these signs when I showed the property. I said no. I think I thanked him for letting me know before hanging up. I went to find my manager, but he had left early for the day. *Okay, so now what?*

I drove to the buyer's house and, obviously, he refused to remove his "subject to satisfactory financing," and he was not going to proceed with the purchase. I didn't blame him at all. But truly, what had happened? This was my first sale.

I drove by the house he was going to buy and sure enough, there were huge red Stop Work Order and No Occupancy Permit signs plastered all over the building. They were everywhere. I knew they weren't there before.

All my buyer wanted was his $5,000 back. *How do I do that*? I wondered. I phoned the listing agent and, in the end, when I followed up on everything, I discovered she had removed all these signs the day I viewed the property with my buyer. I was astounded. I was in shock. My buyer drove by the property numerous times and never saw the signs either, so what was that about?

I found out that my buyer had gone to the city (which is what I should have done) and found out that this building was an absolute disaster with no permits and nothing to authorize raising the house for the two new units on the ground floor.

Not only that, but the tenants were in a dispute with the owners and had filed complaints with the Residential Tenancy Office. I didn't follow up and research that either. I did not include any of the tenancy information in the Contract of Purchase and Sale, which I should have done, and I didn't even ask my buyer if he wanted vacant possession of one of the four units. I should have included a statement like "Information About the Tenants" below.

The Seller warrants the tenant is [____*name*____] who occupies [_*the main floor/ basement/*_
upper floor or__]; the monthly rent is [$_____] including [*list utilities etc.*]; payable on
[*date*]; a security deposit of [$_____] was taken on [*date*]; and the last rental increase was
[*date*]. The Seller warrants the Tenancy is month to month. Any damage/security deposit and any
pet deposit taken will be adjusted between the parties on closing.
The Sellers agree to allow access for any of these parties if required including those already agreed
to in the Access for all Trades Statement.
This subject is for the sole benefit of the Buyers.

The Sellers/Sellers Agents/Representatives/Brokerage warrant and guarantee to arrange, on
reasonable notice, for the purposes of inspection, access to the suite and common areas such as,
but not limited to, the roof, the electrical room, boiler or furnace room, parking areas, storage areas
and recreational areas, at no cost to the Buyers/Buyers Agents/Representatives/ Brokerage.

*For good and valuable consideration of [*One Dollar $1.00 or $*_____] given by the
Buyers and hereby acknowledged and received by the Sellers, the Sellers hereby warrant and
guarantee that their acceptance of this offer will not be withdrawn or revoked prior to the date
for all subjects to be removed. [Seal]
Time shall remain of the essence.
[*Type the word [Seal] exactly as shown*].

[Remember you cannot give out copies of the Report without written consent of the Inspector
and/or Buyers/Sellers]

To think I was trying to be a professional real estate agent. That was ludicrous. I didn't protect my buyer or myself in any way, shape or form. I messed up big time, and I was scared. I wasn't sleeping.

My buyer was Irish and was known to have somewhat of a temper. I was going to take him a case of his favourite beer and some Irish whiskey, but decided against it. He had trusted me and I blew it, from start to finish—but hold on, I still had to get his money back to him. I decided in my wisdom that I would just ask the support staff to return his deposit the next morning. Sure. That didn't happen.

We were a brokerage and holding the money as a stakeholder, so no monies could ever be released without the mutual written consent of the sellers and buyers. The sellers would not sign the release. The $5,000 remained stuck in our trust account for weeks. Finally the sellers did sign the release, and I was able to give the deposit back to the buyer. It was the worst transaction I could ever have gone through, and this was my very first sale with my first buyer.

I remember how, after I told the buyer what the city said on subject removal day, I got back in my car and there on the passenger seat was my official shiny "sold" sticker. I had believed I could just put my own sign up with "sold" on it. No, it doesn't work that way. I would have had to get permission from the sellers through their agent. As I looked down at the "sold" sticker, my eyes were rapidly tearing up. I turned on the windshield wipers, but it wasn't raining outside.

I don't remember ever feeling so sick inside, but it sure taught me a lesson. This would never ever happen again, and I would learn exactly what my job entailed. That meant writing an enforceable Contract of Purchase and Sale that protected all parties. I was just plain sloppy and didn't do my homework at all, and this purchase was definitely out of my level of experience and expertise.

Actually, I had no experience, and definitely no expertise. I should have reported the listing agent to the authorities, but I didn't because she was experienced and well-known, and I was new to the industry. That was wrong of me.

Try picking yourself up after a blow like this and carrying on in real estate. It was probably the hardest thing I ever had to do, and I definitely felt alone taking care of the mess that was all my own doing and my entire fault.

This buyer did buy with me later, so I sincerely thank him for his understanding and patience while I made it my priority to expand my horizons and knowledge level to that of an expert. That I did, but only after another huge mistake, which I'll describe later in this chapter.

Sample Discipline Cases

I decided I should see if anyone else made these types of mistakes with respect to tenants, unauthorized suites, renovations without permits, material latent defects and the like. I really could have been in very serious trouble, but my buyer never filed a complaint. Here are a few samples of what some of our colleagues have had to face with our authorities.

An agent and/or brokerage failed:

- to act with reasonable care and skill, by failing to confirm with the buyers and with the buyers' agent whether the buyers wanted vacant possession of the property. (I never even thought about where my buyer would have lived. What if he wanted me to give notice to one of the tenants? I didn't even ask the questions.)

- to act with reasonable care and skill by not providing to the buyers or their agent any information relating to the tenancies, such as rent, term, security deposits or copies of any tenancy agreements.

- to act in the best interests of the sellers and with reasonable care and skill, by allowing the sellers to confirm vacant possession in the contract knowing that this could not be done since possession was less than 30 days away.

- to act in the best interests of the buyers and with reasonable care and skill, in that he knew that the property was subject to the tenancies and knew that the buyers wanted vacant possession.

- to act in the best interests of his clients and with reasonable care and skill, in that he failed to make sure that the property would not be subject to tenancies.

- by informing the buyers that the property had been rented for one year, when the property had not been rented.

Asking the Tenants to Vacate

I sold a property that was a single-family dwelling with an unauthorized basement suite. The seller was an elderly gentleman who was being transferred into a nursing home. He had a live-in nanny who was an employee, not a tenant, and she was staying in the basement suite.

When the offer was written, the seller said he would deliver vacant possession, so the buyers' agent did not ask us to serve the proper notice to ensure the nanny did vacate. We all just *assumed* (which makes an *ass* out of *u* and *me*) that since the caregiver was an employee hired and paid weekly by the seller, that she would just leave when her employment terminated. Wrong. She did not vacate; she stayed on, claiming she was a tenant.

This taught me a huge lesson: If a nanny, a relative of the sellers, or anyone is staying in a suite in a property, then I will treat that person as a tenant and ensure I follow the tenancy rules to guarantee vacant possession of the entire property.

In the end, the nanny did vacate, but it was a costly lesson. Since then, I have always treated guests in a property as if they were tenants, no matter what they told me.

I know of a similar case where the owner's sister was visiting and staying in a suite in the property, and no one followed the tenancy guidelines treating her as a tenant. The seller had told us she and her sister were both moving to England together. That did not happen, and the sister stayed on, claiming she was a tenant.

This time, there was a large sum of money paid to the sister/tenant in order to get her to leave. The agents for the sellers and buyers shared the cost in order to expedite vacant possession.

Neither of these cases would have happened if all the agents had just done their professional duty. Never assume anything. Put the statement in your Contract of Purchase and Sale asking the sellers to make sure any occupants will vacate.

Your authorities will have a statement similar to this:

> The Sellers will give legal notice to the Tenants to vacate the premises, but only if the Sellers receive the appropriate written request from the Buyers to give such notice in accordance with the requirements of the *[Residential Tenancy Act or the name of your Act]*. The Sellers warrant and guarantee to give a copy of the legal notice served to the tenants to the Buyers or the Buyers' Agents/Representatives/Brokerage *[within 24 hours]* of such notice being officially served to the tenants.

At this time, I also discovered that the description provided on the Tax Report is not the actual legality of a building. Where it states "Actual Use," this only means that the Tax Assessment people know there are three suites or it is a multi-family dwelling. It could even say single-family dwelling with basement suite, but do not ever assume that makes it legal. It does not. It just means the Assessment people know what is in that property. You still must confirm the legality with your local authorities.

Also, do not forget that the assessment value may not be correct. What if the owners have made an appeal to have it reviewed to a lower amount? Be very careful and follow this up.

CHAPTER 12
OFFERS AND COUNTER-OFFERS

Document the date and time the buyers are initially allowing the sellers for acceptance (unless withdrawn in writing with notification to the other party of such revocation prior to notification of its acceptance). If there is a counter, the date and time will probably have to be extended and therefore must be initialled by all parties.

An expired contract cannot be revived. Licensees should draft a new Contract of Purchase and Sale for the parties to sign, or have them sign an extension addendum before the contract expires. A revoked Contract of Purchase and Sale can never be revived either, it has to be rewritten.

For example, when the buyers wrote their initial Contract of Purchase and Sale, they left their offer open until 7:00 p.m. on March 21. If the sellers make any changes to the buyers' original offer, they will sign their acceptance to the offer, but then they will cross off the word *offer* as shown below and they will initial this change. If the buyers accepted the counter as presented, they would initial above as well.

1.
                    Seller's Initial
OFFER: This ~~offer, or~~ Sellers Initial counter-offer, will be open for acceptance until 7:00 o'clock p.m. on March 21ˢᵗ, yr 20_____, [unless withdrawn in writing with notification to the other party].

If now the buyers counter back a second time, they would initial their acceptance of the crossed-off word *offer*, but now they need to extend the date by one day, so they will change the acceptance date from March 21 to March 22 and initial. This now goes back to the sellers for their initials.

2.
                    Seller's Initial
OFFER: This ~~offer, or~~ Seller's Initial counter-offer, will be open for acceptance until 7:00 o'clock p.m. on Buyer's Initial Buyer's Initial March ~~21,~~ 22ⁿᵈ, yr 20_____, Buyer's Initial Buyer's Initial [unless withdrawn in writing with notification to the other party].

The next version indicates that this was a countered contract and that sellers and buyers came to an agreement on or before 7:00 p.m. on March 22.

3.

Seller's Initial

OFFER: This ~~offer, or~~ Seller's Initial counter-offer, will be open for acceptance until 7:00 o'clock p.m. on

Buyer's Initial Buyer's Initial March ~~21,~~ 22nd, yr 20_____, Buyer's Initial Buyer's Initial [unless withdrawn in writing with notification to the other party]. Seller's initial Seller's initial

---

Explanation

When sellers refuse to counter back or even acknowledge an offer because maybe they are offended by the price or for whatever reason, have the sellers sign the form "Thank You for Your Offer or Counter-Offer" (found in the appendix), and at least everyone will be aware that it was in fact presented.

If the sellers counter back to the buyers and the buyers walk, have them sign the same form. It is wise to have copies of this form when you are presenting or countering an offer. It makes everyone relax, because they will know for a fact that their offer/counter-offer was presented to the clients.

The form works for both sellers and buyers who may choose not to deal with an offer in front of them. If either party in the transaction refuses to counter, then you ask them to sign.

Another plus of getting your clients to sign the form is that it gives the listing agents or buyers' agents a second kick at the can. It gives both agents a chance to have their clients sign a counter back rather than signing to say they saw the offer and they don't want to deal with it. It gives you another opportunity, especially since we never want to let an offer die. Encourage them to counter back even if it is at the same price or terms; just try to keep it going.

Never ever let an offer die if you can help it. You must always go back, no matter what. Even if your clients are upset, see if you can convince them to give it one more try. That can mean going back with exactly the same offer that was just rejected.

Never stop. If there was a gap in price, I would even rewrite a counter back from the sellers to the buyers if a few days had passed and we were supposedly at a standstill. If my sellers were wishing they had countered or gone back, what was to stop them? Nothing, and certainly not me.

You are there to help and guide your clients and give them all the professional advice and service you can, and then you can let them decide what to do, but only after you have explained all the pros and cons of not dealing with an offer. You have to follow your clients' lawful instructions, but please do not quit. You might be pleasantly surprised at the final outcome.

It is almost like listing a property with tenants for sale and not asking them to be your clients. Did you ask them if they wanted to buy that property, or would they be interested in buying something else?

CHAPTER 13
SUBJECTS REMOVED, FULFILLED OR WAIVED

This is an example of deleting the subjects, but it is very important that you use the correct wording. If they did perform the subject you must be very specific and use the word *remove* or *fulfill*. If they did not perform the subject, then make sure you use the word *waive*. These removals/waivers can all be on the same page.

If you use the word *waive*, everyone understands that the buyers chose not to complete that task and just let it go. They didn't do what was allowed and chose just to waive it.

Suggestion: If you are using one of your industry's amendment forms where the preprinted heading contains the words "to remove/fulfill or waive," make sure you specify exactly what the buyers chose to do regarding each and every subject. It can make a difference if there are problems down the road.

Examples

To **REMOVE** the following subjects, namely, **OR** To **FULFILL** the following subjects, namely:

This Contract of Purchase and Sale is subject to finalization of the preapproved mortgage *[in the amount of $_____]* on or before *[date]*.
This subject is for the sole benefit of the Buyers.
This Contract of Purchase and Sale is subject to the Buyers, on or before [date], at the Buyers' expense, obtaining and approving an inspection report [or professional inspection] against any defects [whose cumulative cost of repair exceeds $_____ and] which reasonably may adversely affect the property's use or value.
This subject is for the sole benefit of the Buyers.

To **WAIVE** the following subjects, namely:

This Contract of Purchase and Sale is subject to the Buyers at their expense confirming that there are no pre-existing issues or conditions that would prevent the Buyers from obtaining insurance coverage including but not limited to content, liability, specified perils on or before *[date]*. This subject is for the sole benefit of the Buyers.

Do not add any other wording such as "This is now a firm and binding Contract of Purchase and Sale" or "The deposit has been received."

There are two times a Contract of Purchase and Sale can never be revived.

1. **Subject Removal | Dates/Times Have Expired:** Agents must redo a new Contract of Purchase and Sale for the parties to sign if the subject removal dates have expired, or have them sign an extension addendum *before* the Contract of Purchase and Sale expires.

2. **Revocation:** If a Contract of Purchase and Sale is ever revoked, you can never revive it. It is dead. You must write a new contract.

This reinforces strongly that you must always pay strict attention to any and all timelines involved, including when deposits are expected.

CHAPTER 14
CHANGING AN ACCEPTED CONTRACT

There can be many reasons for a change in an accepted contract. Maybe the completion, possession and adjustment dates need to be changed. The first sample here is one in which the clients demand that the requested change must be agreed to. What if the sellers will not agree to the changes? Does that mean your offer is dead?

What if there was another offer waiting in the wings? Does that mean your offer is collapsed and the secondary offer comes into play? Not necessarily, because it will depend on the wording used. Whenever you change an already accepted contract, you must always remember to do three things:

1. Restate the consideration, or it could just be considered a gratuitous problem: "For good and valuable consideration, the Buyers and Sellers mutually agree …" or "For good and valuable consideration of [One Dollar $1.00 or $_____] given by the Buyers and hereby acknowledged and received by the Sellers …."

2. Add in "Time shall remain of the essence."

3. Add in "All other terms and conditions remain the same and in full force and effect."

Here is a sample for date changes. The first sample is just restating the consideration; the second includes payment to enforce the consideration.

For good and valuable consideration, the Sellers and Buyers mutually agree that the
        Completion Date of [_state Date_] will now be [_state Date_]
        Possession Date of [_state Date_] will now be [_state Date_]
        Adjustment Date of [_state Date_] will now be [_state Date_].
Time shall remain of the essence.
All other terms and conditions remain the same and in full force and effect.
[Do you want a date and time for everyone to sign this change, and what happens if all parties won't sign it]?

For good and valuable consideration of [One Dollar $1.00 or $_____] given by the Buyers and hereby acknowledged and received by the Sellers, the Sellers and Buyers mutually agree that the

        Completion Date of [state Date] will now be [state Date]

        Possession Date of [state Date] will now be [state Date]

        Adjustment Date of [state Date] will now be [state Date].

Time shall remain of the essence.

All other terms and conditions remain the same and in full force and effect.

[Do you want a date and time for everyone to sign this change and what happens if all parties won't sign it]?

Please make sure you are following the rules. Do not lose a transaction because you forgot or were just too tired that day or in a hurry. Do not take shortcuts either. You are working for and protecting your clients. It is your duty. It is your responsibility.

Do you want a date and time for everyone to sign this change, and what happens if all parties won't sign it? It seems that we are not leaving these requested changes open for a specific time and date. How long is this requested change in effect? It is up to you whether to insert this or not.

When Approval Is Not Required

Your clients may not particularly care if the other parties agree to their request. They are willing to ask the sellers or buyers to agree to a change to the accepted contract, but if one of the parties won't sign it, they will still proceed to completion. Sometimes this does happen, and the clients just want to see if everyone could come to a mutual agreement for a change.

This is definitely not legal advice from me—remember, I am not a lawyer, I am an agent just like you—but you could definitely check the following example out with your legal people and legislation.

I sincerely thank Mr. Jeff Scouten, who is a founding partner of the Vancouver, British Columbia, law firm of Henshall Scouten, for the following sample amendment asking for a change but not opening up the Contract of Purchase and Sale.

In consideration for a payment to be made of $1.00 [One Dollar] and other good and valuable consideration, the *[Sellers/Buyers]* hereby request the *[Sellers'/Buyers']* agreement to modify the terms of the Contract of Purchase and Sale as follows:

1.
2.
3.

[Do you want to add this in?]
This amendment is open for acceptance by the *[Sellers/Buyers]* until *[Date and time].*

In making this request, the *[Sellers/Buyers]* do not in any way repudiate or decline to honour any of the terms or conditions of the Contract of Purchase and Sale, and the *[Sellers/Buyers]* are free to decline this request if they wish, in which case the terms and conditions of the Contract of Purchase and Sale will remain binding on the parties without change.

If the *[Sellers/Buyers]* are willing to agree to modify the terms of the Contract of Purchase and Sale as set out herein, then by the parties signing this Amendment in the spaces provided below they hereby agree to modify the Contract of Purchase and Sale as set out above, and do further agree that:

1. Time remains of the essence;
2. The party to whom the consideration recited above is payable acknowledges having received such consideration; and
3. The terms and conditions of the Contract of Purchase and Sale, except as specifically modified by this Addendum, remain in full force and effect.

See the above amendments in the appendix: "Date Changes | Statement" and "Not Altering the Contract of Purchase and Sale."

CHAPTER 15
TURNING IN YOUR DOCUMENTS

You have to turn in all contracts and paperwork to your brokerage immediately after a contract is accepted, whether you have a deposit or not. These are the rules, so please follow them. Do not wait until subject removal. Do not wait for a deposit.

As soon as the contract is accepted, you must give all the paperwork to your brokerage, including the transaction record sheet. As further documentation is received, you must turn it in to your managing broker accordingly. You must also keep your managing broker informed of anything relevant to your transactions.

Here are a few examples of where some agents did not follow these rules, and then some examples of where some decided to operate independent of the brokerage they were working at. Don't do any of these. It's just not worth it! Honestly, do you really want to face our authorities?

Sample Discipline Cases

An agent and/or brokerage failed to:

- provide copies of the transaction and related documents regarding the contract to the brokerage promptly.

- provide the managing broker with a copy of the trading records regarding his attempted purchase.

- immediately notify the managing broker when the deposit called for in the contract was not received.

- disclose his status as a licensee and his interest in trade regarding his attempted purchase of lands.

- provide the managing broker with copies of the trading records.

141

- provide the managing broker with a copy of a contract.

- keep the managing broker informed of the real estate services they were providing.

- promptly provide to the managing broker all general records and trading records including the contract.

- promptly provide to the brokerage the trade records for the intended sale.

- act honestly and exercise reasonable care and skill to ensure the brokerage was aware of the arrangement made with the seller and in entering into such an agreement.

- promptly provide to his managing broker the original or a copy of trading records, provide a copy of the offer or the contract, and keep the managing broker informed of trading services being provided.

- promptly provide the managing broker the original or copies of all trading records until after the subjects had been removed.

- promptly provide the managing broker with a copy of the Disclosure of Interest in Trade, Disclosure of Remuneration, and Assignment Agreement.

- promptly provide the managing broker with a copy of all incorporated documents.

- promptly provide the managing broker with a copy of all tenancy agreements and documentation, including separate leases.

Comments

Our authorities require that you turn in a contract to your brokerage as soon as an offer is accepted. You must not hold the paperwork until subject removal or until a deposit is received, or for any other reason. During the course of the counter-offers and/or subject removals, you must turn in the additional paperwork as received and required, so again, do not hold any documents until you have a firm Contract of Purchase and Sale.

It is wise if you turn in all the papers you have in your possession. This could include items like disclosures, the Property Disclosure Statement, the Title Search, proof of signing authority, rental statements, notices asking the tenants to vacate, leases or rent rolls, written instructions from the sellers—everything.

It is of enormous help if you also turn in the full REALTOR® MLS® printout of the listing. This is significant to the managing broker who reviews your Contract of Purchase and Sale.

Stay Out of Real Estate Jail

Let's say there was an unauthorized suite showing in the REALTOR® remarks. Then the broker can confirm that you have the required predisclosures and the date they were acknowledged by all parties to the contract. If you forgot this disclosure and it is prior to subject removal, the managing broker—by having all the documents as early as possible—can help you correct this information in an amendment.

If you follow my suggestions in this book, the odds of you forgetting any types of disclosures and/or documents are greatly minimized or even impossible, because they are referred to in the 32 statements that could be in most of your Contracts of Purchase and Sale.

As you know, it is much easier to correct errors prior to, for example, subjects being removed. So if your managing broker has your contract and paperwork, you can receive assistance in executing an amendment with the precise wording required. Please always try to turn in the full REALTOR® MLS® printout. If ever there was a problem, say five years later, if you had turned in a complete contract and all paper relating to the specific transaction, at least you would have a backup with your brokerage's retained files.

True Story

An agent moved during the course of this mentioned five-year period and somehow lost the original backup copies and his entire file. Thank goodness he was incredibly detailed and made sure the brokerage had a full copy of every item, including phone calls. This same scenario occurred when an agent's computer crashed and this individual did not have a backup. The office did have everything on file.

143

CHAPTER 16
MASTERING YOUR CRAFT—GETTING THIS DOWN TO A FINE ART

Consumers are far more empowered today than ever before, especially with the information superhighway available to them. You have to demonstrate your commitment to your clients by counselling and protecting them. One of the most effective ways is by creating and mastering the art of writing the perfect Contract of Purchase and Sale.

You have to discipline yourself and strive for perfection. The good news is that it is all here in this book for you to take advantage of and to implement into your business plan. You can just retype the clauses and phrases onto the forms provided by your authority or set them up any way you wish. These can be paperless or hard copies or both.

Prioritize a specific appointment with yourself now, which means *today*, and begin setting up these resources in a place and a format that suits you and your personal style. Whatever method you select, that is the one you will use from this day forward. You must be consistent so you do not ever forget anything.

You only have to do this once, if you take your time, and after that you can begin building relationships that will lead to a ton of business in the future. Don't forget to relate specifically to the legislation in your market area when you are entering the information for each topic.

Take the information from the book and retype it yourself, or go to my website at www.barbarabellolsen.com, where it is all pretyped and prepared in word-processing documents for you. You do not have to type anything; it is all done for you. Just edit, cut, copy and paste.

The website contains incredible details on many other significant real estate requirements, including over 700 pages of sample pretyped clauses and phrases, pretyped addendums, sample thank-you notes, questionnaires, checklists and forms that I will outline for you at the end of this book.

It contains a much broader spectrum of information than I could fit in the book, and it even offers an unmatched step-by-step guide to creating and implementing the Ultimate Buyers' Presentation Package. This is the Cadillac of any buyers' presentation.

Start with setting up your Contracts of Purchase and Sale, and you must begin by exercising new habits, learning and creating new skills, and ending up exactly where you want to be: as a successful and prosperous business entrepreneur.

You must show your prospects that you are the very best, the most professional and the most respected agent for the job. You want them to hire you, and by using the Ultimate Buyers' Presentation Package, you will convince them to do just that.

You will make a positive and professional connection with your clients, who will be eager to employ you. The vacancy is filled. You showed them the key benefits of having you represent them, and you made an incredible, significant and powerful impact on their final decision to hire you.

We have reviewed in depth the primary clauses and phrases, specifically:

- the 32 statements that could be in most contracts

- the Famous Five

- the property specifics.

You must focus on these each and every time you write an offer. You cannot afford to forget anything. You must be disciplined and follow the same format with each Contract of Purchase and Sale that you write. You must be consistent.

We've gone over such items as:

- offers and counter-offers

- removing the subjects

- changing an accepted Contract of Purchase and Sale

- turning in your documents.

Don't forget that whenever you are preparing a contract, you must pretend it is you and your family buying the property. This helps you think about everything and ask yourself, *What would I want to know if I was purchasing this property?* If you have any concerns, no matter how small, it is critical that you make the statements into subjects. It is a red flag.

Do you honestly know anyone else who explains the *real* process of what is actually involved in buying or selling a property? This is huge, and you should use it to your advantage.

From my research, there are two major frustrations expressed by the public about real estate agents.

1. Buyers are seldom advised of the process of buying, including clauses, phrases, subjects and property specifics that should or could be in their contracts and beneficial to them.

2. Communication and follow-up are lacking. Buyers said we are often missing in action.

> All the surveys confirm the above two statements, and buyers are adamant that they often have no idea what to expect when they do find their dream home. They too need a blueprint as to how the entire buying process works.

True Story

I remember when I first started in real estate, I was speaking with one of the most respected and ethical agents, and she gave me some very vital and factual information. We were in a counter-offer situation, and my buyers were upset with some of the sellers' requests.

This agent was aware that I was new to the business and told me that I should have prewarned my buyers about these items and what the sellers wanted. They should not have been a shock or surprise to my buyers. She said she disclosed the sellers' wishes to me, and I should have relayed the information to my buyers in a clear and specific manner as soon as I became aware of them. No surprises. No shocks.

That's when she told me that surprises are only for anniversary parties, birthday parties and other special occasions.

I never forgot her words of wisdom. From that moment on, I always asked as many questions as possible of the listing agent, and I definitely passed the information on to my buyers very quickly. (A few samples of these questionnaires are in the appendix, and there are many more questionnaires and checklists on my website.)

She was also the agent who taught me the words, "We sell dirt." We do not sell appliances, remove rubbish, or clean carpets. This came about because I had asked her if all the appliances were included and working. She was emphatic when replying, "Barbara, we sell dirt." I never forgot her words or the tone of her voice.

After the transaction finally came together, I did mail her a handwritten thank-you note with two business cards, not just because I sincerely appreciated her advice, but also because that was the very day I stopped buying microwaves, paying for garbage removal, and cleaning carpets.

Communication

Below I will review how to present the components of a contract to your buyers, beginning at the onset of the relationship right up to and including the moving date, not just when they are ready to make an offer on their dream home.

Buyers feel we just disappear, we don't communicate, we don't tell them what's happening. I made sure that was a number-one priority on my list. I have even phoned people to tell them that nothing has happened, there are no new properties for sale today, but I will still keep in touch. That's a tough thing to do, believe me. I let them vent, but at least I did talk or see them. Stay connected. They need that from us. They expect that from us.

So do our colleagues. Let them know what your buyers thought of the property; let them know where the offer is sitting. Their people are also waiting to hear something. Stay in touch with everyone and stay in touch often. "No news is good news" is *not* the answer in our profession. Keep in touch daily if need be.

E-mails are not personal at all. Even if the buyers said their preferred method of contact was e-mail, that doesn't apply to just keeping in touch. You must be face to face or on the phone with them, and often. Don't lose them now; that would be crazy. They are your clients, so you want to always remind them why they did in fact choose the best person to work for them.

There are no excuses, including "I just don't have time" or "I have nothing to say." Yes, you do have time. You make the time and you listen to them. Let them express their concerns, if that is what they need to do. *Listen* and *silent* have the same letters. Coincidence? Did you know this? Think about it! *Seriously, think about it.* I remember being told this years ago. Remember this one! We learn by *listen*ing, and that means being *silent*. Actually hear what your clients are asking or telling you.

When they are ready to write, they will be so darn prepared and excited that you will be their knight in shining armour. They will know what to expect and why you are doing what you are doing. They will be so thrilled they chose you over everyone else.

Your personalized service involves helping your clients understand the entire buying process—showing properties, reviewing and explaining the statements and subjects, and negotiating the best price and terms. You'll be educating them every step of the way.

Remember, we are a real estate family, and even though we are a competitive family, we work together to everyone's advantage. We need each other to grow ourselves, our business and our bank accounts.

You aren't really in sales as such, you are in the service industry, and that means doing it properly and doing it properly the very first time. You deliver service that is first-class, and you possess extraordinary skills. You deliver ethical, honest and sincere value to your clients and to your colleagues. It is important.

One other valuable point is that your colleagues will thank you for such a well-written and thorough Contract of Purchase and Sale. You will be known in the industry as a professional, and your colleagues will enjoy working with you. They won't have to rewrite your contracts. They know you can do your job and you know what you are doing. You care about your clients, customers and colleagues. You are good at what you do. You are proud of what you do.

Many agents are reviewing the 32 statements and the Famous Five when they first commence a relationship with their buyers, and they continue explaining these and the critical steps of the buying process throughout the entire working partnership. You must immediately set appointments with yourself to initiate setting up the art of mastering and writing your contracts. Procrastination is not allowed. Yes, it is time-consuming, but think about this: Once you have written it, or copied and pasted everything, you are done.

You are the captain of your ship, and you can set sail to meet as many more clients and customers as possible every day. The more people you meet, the more business you will have. If you are a seasoned agent, reshape the way you have been doing business. Grasp the modern and unique concepts and suggestions in this book and use them to make yourself absolutely indispensable. If you are new to our wonderful profession, start off on the right foot by following these guidelines.

I sincerely wish I had something like this when I was first in the industry—a manual of what to do, how to do it and why I was doing it. You will always be learning, but you must continue your education, listen and learn, and keep on learning in order to keep growing in every phase of your life and career. Knowledge is power. Excellence is a habit.

I also learned that no matter how savvy your clients say they are, just pretend that they do not know anything about real estate, and then with your professional, ethical, open and honest communication explain how the process works and what each party's options are so that they will be able to make informed decisions. I would be precise, to the point, quiet, calm, reassuring and thorough. That way, when something came up they didn't quite understand, we just reviewed it without embarrassing anyone, including me.

Also, always repeat a person's name as often as you can. Well, not every second sentence, but we all love being referred to by name. Not only that, if you are anything like me and forget people's names, this will help you remember. I often associate something with the name to help me remember it. Yes, it might be funny or rhyme or be a little rude—anything so I don't forget. No, don't call them names, call them *by* name.

From the onset of the relationship, you want to establish rapport and credibility. You want to leave no stone unturned so that when it is time to make an offer, you will have eased their worries and they'll know just how it all works. They'll know you will protect them, they will be impressed, and they won't be scared or back out at this critical time because they are unsure of what they are getting into. They already know, thanks to you and all your preplanning and pre-explaining.

Remember I asked you if you would feel proud to show someone the last contract you wrote? Well, if you take the time and energy to set everything up as I have shown you, I would bet money that the next contract you write will be something you are proud of. But it won't happen if you don't take the time to set up and organize the way that you do business.

Getting Organized

The good news is that you don't have to figure it out; my system does that for you. Set up all your statements that could be in most contracts. Follow this with the subjects (the Famous Five) and again set them up the simplest way for you to use in your contracts when a buyer is ready to write an offer. You can enter them all separate under each heading, use the addendums or go with whatever is the best method for you. For example:

Subject: Financing

- Finalization of the Preapproved Mortgage

- Satisfactory Financing

- Specific Details

- Can the Sellers Clear the Title?

    Subject: Fire Property Insurance

- Residential

    Subject: Inspection of the Property

- Residential

    Subject and/or Statement: Property Specifics

The Property Disclosure Statement and the Title Search are now statements in most of your Contracts of Purchase and Sale.

Suggestion: You could set up the four possible financing subjects on individual addendums, and the same with the insurance and inspection. If you put them on addendums, just use the appropriate page and add it to your Contract of Purchase and Sale. You would then follow with any property specifics applicable to the property the buyers are interested in. Others just put them all together and edit, cut, copy and paste the one they need and add it to their contract.

After these are all entered and amended to suit your authorities and legislation, you are done. You never have to redo them unless it means leaving one of them out for a particular offer or your legislation changes.

It is very important that you keep your contracts in the same order every time. It also eases any nervousness you may have, especially if the clients are chitchatting in your ear. You won't forget anything.

Think about this for a minute. It isn't costing you any money to set up the contracts, statements, subjects, clauses and phrases, since they are all predone for you. It will take you time to originally set them up, but then you are done.

The property specifics you need for the particular property you are writing an offer on are in the clauses and phrases section and/or under the forms section on my website to help you with any disclosures or notices you may have to use. (There is also a form "Disclaimers | Samples" you may need, so make sure to review it.)

If you are not quite ready to use the information on my website, then you would just insert your authority-recommended clauses and phrases for any of the property specifics. For now, though, use the 32 statements and the Famous Five and set up your Contracts of Purchase and Sale using these. You can't go wrong!

Cross-reference any separate disclosures and pieces of paper in your contract. If you are going to use my system, then the statements, subjects and clauses already do acknowledge receipt of any separate documents and disclosure.

Remember, after you have set up your system, you never have to do it again and you can spend your time meeting with clients and devoting your time to other aspects of your job that will create more business for you. By being organized, you will have confidence in yourself; that will be immediately apparent to your clients, and word will spread. You could easily have enough time to write three, four or more contracts per day, and then you really will be on the road to success.

Don't forget to collect your reward. I am truly a fan of goal-setting, but that is for another book. I do believe, though, that you must always reward yourself after any accomplishment, no matter how small. I think you should visualize in detail what you want or need once you have the entire program in place and up and running.

I really am excited for you to start on your new journey. Get ready for your career to take off. There is nothing to stop you; you can do anything you want, so go do it! Have fun too. Be proud and represent your clients to the very best of your abilities. Work with your colleagues, communicate often and be the leader of the pack.

From the amount of e-mails I have been receiving and the questions over the years of teaching, I've realized just how concerned our agents are with finding an easier way to do their business. I took a poll and found out that the average length of time to write a contract was four to five hours. This did not always include reviewing the clauses and phrases and the final prepared Contract of Purchase and Sale. If that is the case, these agents could never prepare three, four or five contracts in one day.

Some agents were able to do a fairly straightforward contract in an hour or less because they had the statements already prepared and just copied them into the needed contract. Then some told me that they often forgot a clause or two and their order of preparing the contract was all over the map, with a few statements that all parties would agree to and then a few subjects to protect their buyers and then a few more statements. They had no checklist or method to follow, and then with all the requirements for predisclosures, they were just overwhelmed.

Not only that, often the buyers were sitting with them and talking away while the agent was trying to prepare the contract. They were very concerned and wanted a method including checklists of what to do step-by-step.

One day you may pay the price for forgetting something or not being able to prove that the disputed item was covered in full with your clients. Most of our transactions go off without problems, but when someone does decide to complain it can cost you dearly and not just money, but the stress, the embarrassment and the time you will spend replying to complaints and defending yourself.

Consequently, I felt it was time to write this book and share my amazing and easy procedures so no one ever faces this type of fear and trauma again. That was it—the inspiration for this book. I have put my whole heart and life into writing it, and I am thrilled to be able to help you have the most successful business possible.

By using what is in the book and once you set it up, you could easily do four, five or more contracts in one day even if the buyers are chatting in your ear. You would have the contracts all prewritten and ready to go. Select the statements you need, the subjects and then add in the property specifics. It's done.

I seriously believe you can more than triple or quadruple your business and your bank account. You will be incredibly successful. This is because you will now know what you have to do and how to do it. You will reach your ultimate goal of crossing the finish line with an exceptional enforceable contract and fantastic, happy relationships that will lead to more referrals and more business for you.

By having your contracts ready, you will be able to spend the majority of your days prospecting and meeting new clients. This creates more business for you. What more could you ask for? Yes, your bank account will increase too, because you now have time to meet and greet all the people. You are full of dynamite and ready—more than ready. Just light that flame.

I sincerely hope you will grasp the ideas and suggestions in this book.

Finally do not forget, your name is your reputation. Protect it and promote it.

You have mastered the art of writing a contract no matter how complex or involved it is, you offer stellar service, you outshine everyone, and you really are on the road to success.

Be inspired to be the very best, simplify your business and your life, and strive to cross that finish line with a burning goal of accomplishment.

You too will be fiercely proud to be a real estate agent.

So go out and create some business, because when your clients are ready to write, *so are you!*

barbarabellolsen@shaw.ca
www.barbarabellolsen.com

CONCLUSION

The Buyers: Mr. and Mrs. Snerdle

I was sitting at my computer putting all my contracts in order so that I would always be prepared the minute someone wanted to make an offer.

The phone rang. I answered as quickly as possible and remembered to smile.

"Good morning, this is Barbara Bell-Olsen."

"Hello, Ms. Bell-Olsen, my name is Mr. Mortimer J. Snerdle." Now I am stifling a chuckle, but I notice he used "Mr." and he specifically stated his middle initial; that's an instruction to call him Mr. Snerdle. He also called me Ms. Bell-Olsen.

"My wife, Gertrude, and I are thinking it might be the right time to buy a property. Our friends Mr. Hank and Mrs. Gladys Happy told us how you helped them and suggested we give you a call."

"That's great, Mr. Snerdle." I love Hank Happy and his wife, Glad Happy. It's hard to resist laughing at their names, but I've trained myself never to do so, no matter how goofy I think someone's name sounds. Maybe after I hang up the phone I can giggle in private.

"Well, good morning, Mr. Snerdle, and please call me Barb."

Now Mr. Snerdle and Barb chitchat, and the goal is to set a date, time and location to meet. I want to make sure I can meet with both Mr. and Mrs. Snerdle together.

Don't ever call people by their first names until they invite you to do so. This is just common courtesy and etiquette. Notice he even referred to the Happys as Mr. and Mrs., so that reinforced that this is a gentleman who cares about respect, etiquette and politeness. I would lose any relationship with him the minute I referred to him by his first name, Mortimer. He has not given me permission to do so.

You should have all the following documentation readily available, either paperless or hard copy, for times when someone does call to work with you. The entire list, with simple straightforward explanations and how to put it all together, is on my website, so this is only to give you an idea of what you can do and what is available for you to own. You will always need three colour-coded master sets of files containing all the documents and information you will ever need:

- one for sellers

- one for buyers

- one for sales contracts/documents, including listing contracts/documents.

A second set of these master files should be in the trunk of your vehicle, even if you work paperless. What if your computer crashed and you needed some information or a particular form, including disclosure forms, the Contract of Purchase and Sale, wording of your 32 statements that could be in most of your contracts, and the Famous Five? I personally had this happen, so I always had hard copies in my car trunk, just in case.

As Mr. Snerdle and I are conversing, I reach for my buyers' questionnaire; if it wasn't handy, I would just grab a piece of paper and ask Mr. Snerdle the questions I want answers to from memory. I really hope the form is accessible, as it makes my job that much easier. I want to follow my prepared questionnaire checklist. I want to get as much information as I possibly can, and I want to sound professional, all the while showing Mr. Snerdle how much I care about working with him.

Remember, he called me on a referral from Mr. and Mrs. Happy, so he is in effect interviewing me to see if I seem suitable to go for a face-to-face meeting. First impressions do matter. Accordingly, I must portray my extraordinary skills and my personal marketing plan to satisfy his needs.

Consumers want to know what's in it for them. How would Mr. Snerdle benefit from hiring me as his real estate agent? I want him to understand that I have impeccable skills and knowledge and a sincere interest in his needs, and I will focus all my energies on assisting and protecting him and Mrs. Snerdle.

I get all their contact information and everything I can. If they want me to communicate via fax, and some people still do, I remember to ask if they have to turn the fax on prior to my sending them anything.

I am still grinning from ear to ear with an upbeat voice emitting enthusiasm and excitement for my new clients. There is absolutely no doubt in my mind that I will win them over and end up working with them, but only if I like them too. I am quite particular about who I work with. I have learned my lesson. No doubt at all.

I am smiling all the while talking with him. I am trying to find out whatever I can, and the more the better. Always let the prospective client talk as much as possible, and jot everything down. Remember, *listen* and *silent* have the same letters.

Once my appointment is scheduled and the call is finished, I drop anything else I was doing—unless, of course, I was writing another Contract of Purchase and Sale. I then diarize and enter the appointment in my Day-Timer and/or on my computer, cell calendar or instant-message alert.

I have a prepared Buyer's Information Record Sheet form that I would then fill in with all my notes, including my personal thoughts during the conversation. This could include his tone of voice and my initial feelings about him, and I would make it a priority to mark in the file with a red pen that I must only call him Mr. Snerdle.

This is the actual form I will take to my first meeting. Depending on how you set up your files, you may want to scan and put a copy of this in a new file on your computer, or set up a hard copy of the file, or both.

If you are meeting new clients at their residence or any other location, just as a quick reminder, let others know when and where you are going, especially since this is the first face-to-face contact. Also, run their names through the computer and see if you can find out anything about them or if there are any reported warnings. It is just a precaution. Also, let your family know you will be late for dinner if that is the case.

If the Snerdles have an e-mail or fax, I send them a thank-you right away, minutes after I have finished the phone conversation, and confirm the date, time and location for our first meeting.

Maybe the Snerdles only have a fax. That is fine too, but I always attach the transmission record sheet to the original fax and double-check that it actually was transmitted, the number of pages sent and received, and that there was not an error or the line was busy. Make sure it doesn't say zero pages sent or something similar. Confirm that the cover sheet states the correct total number of pages being faxed. Put these in your presentation package.

During my conversation with Mr. Snerdle, I did ask if they had a fax, and I confirmed if it is always accessible or do they have to turn it on. I wrote this in my notes when speaking with Mr. Snerdle.

Suggestion: Always send a prepared return fax cover sheet preaddressed to you and completed so the receivers of your original do not have to make a separate cover sheet. They will appreciate this, so don't forget to include it when you are transmitting the initial information.

I personally would always send a handwritten thank-you note even if it would arrive after I met with them in person. You would have made the appointment as soon as possible to meet with both of them.

You must always have a sense of urgency in our profession. That doesn't mean pushing people, it means giving more than what they are expecting. You have to try to always be one step ahead.

Remember to always add a PS (postscript) to any notes and put something with impact. It is proven that people read it and remember it more than the actual note itself, so give it some punch. Maybe you put something that was said while you were on the phone, but make it personal and pack a wallop. It is your grand finale to the thank-you. It can be something you want them to do or look at.

Portray enthusiasm and sincerity. Be excited. Personalize the envelope by using a postage stamp, not a postage meter. People notice this. Always enclose two business cards.

How did the conversation end? Even if Mr. Snerdle gave me permission to call him Mortimer, I have not yet met Gertrude, so I will address them as Mr. and Mrs. Snerdle. Never overstep the etiquette rules.

Now it is time to decide when to send information about you and your brokerage. You will know if this is the appropriate time or not depending on what was stated in your conversation. If you felt during the conversation that it would be very important for the clients to have information about you and your brokerage, you might want to consider sending a full package by courier along with your thank-you note. Have the thank-you note in a separate envelope clipped to the top of your package, and then put the entire set of documents in one large envelope. Always include two business cards.

I give Hank and Gladys Happy a phone call now, not in a day or two, and thank them. They will probably be able to give me even more information on Mortimer J. and Gertrude Snerdle, which could be of great help, so I let them do the talking while I make notes. I then follow up and send a handwritten thank-you note.

Again, portray enthusiasm and sincerity. Be excited. Don't even think of asking for more business from the people who gave you this referral. Just send a genuine honest thank-you. That is the purpose of your phone call and note. They will appreciate it. Again, personalize the envelope by using a postage stamp, not a postage meter. People notice this. Always enclose two business cards.

Hank and Gladys Happy are my previous clients and they referred me, so I long ago received their consent to address any information or thank-you notes to them using their first names in the salutation. I make a copy of the thank-you note and put it in my master file.

Suggestion: On my website, I have prepared a number of sample thank-you notes to save you from having to think of what to say. They are only ideas and are included for your convenience.

If you have the worst handwriting in the world, maybe your partner or someone could handwrite the note for you, or print it if there isn't time, but never type a thank-you note. The writing should be consistent. You must jot down what you want your ghostwriter to copy; it has to come from you.

This is the start of building a relationship with your client.

Make sure you mail the notes on the day you actually speak with the contact. If it is a buyer, drive by where they live so you will be better prepared for your meeting with them. If they are in a parking-meter area, you will make sure you have money for the meter, although you should carry a roll of coins in your glove box just in case. Also, check the length of time allowed on the meters so you will know how long you can park there.

Before meeting with the Snerdles, I go on the computer to MLS® and check their address. If they own their home, I see what the activity is or was on their property, and always attach the tax report.

I try to think outside the box, too. What if they don't own it? When I meet the Snerdles, I could ask them if their home was for sale, would they want to buy it? Maybe I can contact the registered owners. Who knows?

See if anything is going on or has been going on with your prospective clients. It is just more in-depth information for you when you meet with them. Add this information to your master file.

What if Mr. and Mrs. Snerdle are tenants at their current address? When they buy, they will be giving notice. Maybe the owners are tired of renting the property out? After the Snerdles have purchased, I might want to follow up and contact the owners to see if they want to sell. I would never do this before I know the Snerdles have given notice to vacate, however.

I have set up the Ultimate Buyers' Presentation Package on my website for you to use when you meet with buyers. They will be impressed with you and your presentation. Even you will be impressed. It is all ready for you to edit, cut, copy and paste. It's easy.

There are two packages—one master copy for you and one for the buyers—and then there are two sets of index cover sheets for you to copy and paste if you want to use them. You just pick the one you prefer. Here are a few samples that you can add to or edit as you see fit:

- Buyers | Questions and Answers | From the Public

- My Personal Information and Website Information

- Cover Sheet for File | Buyers | Must Haves and Would Like

- Showings | Buyers' Comments

- Why You Should Work with Me | I Am Your Professional Consultant and Advisor

This list is not all-encompassing, as there are numerous other items and headings of material you would want to include, but it is all available for you to choose from, including sample wording.

It is startling how impressed your clients will be when they see your professional organizational skills and that you truly do care about them and what *they* want and need. They will be amazed at your eye for detail and extraordinary service just for them.

All they really do care about is *what can you do for them*, so now you have surpassed their expectations in actions and not just in words. You have to sincerely feel this way, because if you try to fake it they will know and you probably shouldn't be working with them.

Remember, you want them to hire you, but you have to want to work with them too. You do have a choice. Don't let one set of clients ruin your reputation. Walk away if you are not comfortable.

Arriving at the Appointment

When meeting with new clients, dress appropriately. You are a business professional. First impressions really do matter. I always wear my brokerage name badge when I personally meet clients, and I have the REALTOR® pin on my coat.

I always wear my identification proudly, except in the few circumstances I already mentioned, but in a face-to-face meeting I want to make sure it's visible when I take my coat off. Don't be a secret agent.

Never be late. It is just plain rude. I always arrive at least half an hour in advance and wait outside. This gives me time to review my thoughts, get all my materials together and scan through my prepared packages once more.

I double-check that the correct information is in the presentation package for the buyers and that I didn't accidentally include anything from my personal master file. That would not be good, since it has my personal notes, comments and thoughts.

Because I have already driven here the day before, I know where the parking is and whether I need money for meters.

Ring the doorbell and introduce yourself. You will know if you should shake hands or not. From my phone conversation and being called Ms. Bell-Olsen, I am going to ask them to please call me Barb. Think common courtesy and etiquette.

Always be diplomatic. Do you take your shoes off? Do you use your shoe protectors?

Once seated, after making sure it is an appropriate location to have a serious conversation with them and also so everyone can make notes, you can then decide whether to hand them two business cards or put them on the table. To some it is a sign of respect if you hand them your business cards using both your hands.

Are you truly prepared for your job interview? That is what you are doing.

Now the normal chitchat will prevail, and I make it a point to reference Mr. and Mrs. Happy, the folks who referred me.

Most people will offer you a beverage. This is not the time to have a beer or a glass of wine, although you probably would love one. I often brought bottled water, and no, it wasn't vodka concealed as water, although sometimes I think it should have been or wished it had been.

I use the Ultimate Buyers' Presentation Package, which I will review step by step. I've brought along a copy personalized for Mr. Snerdle and one for Mrs. Snerdle.

Your presentation to prospective buyers has to be from the heart, factual and honest. Emphasize that you really want to work with these clients and why you want to work with them. You have to be proud, professional, honest and ethical, and portray these qualities to your clients.

Suggestion: Be patient, take your time, and set this up as the classiest and most professional package. After all, you are creating a masterpiece. Your buyers will be in awe.

You have to outshine your competition, and believe me, you can do this very easily. You will also be leaving their copy with them, so make it a showstopper. Who knows if they will show it to their business acquaintances, family and friends? You only get the one chance to make a good impression, and this is where you want to do it.

My personal master copy is a three-ring binder with a dynamic, unique and impressive-looking front and back cover. I had binders printed professionally with what I wanted on them, and I had a set of index tabs printed so I knew where everything was when I was reviewing my material with buyers. Do you realize how much of an impact this has? Believe me, the buyers notice.

Maybe the front and back cover sheets are in your personal colours. You want to make sure that what you use is the same for everything; it must be consistent, as you are building a brand for yourself, including your mission statement if you decide to have one. Keep it with your colours and in the same format you use for all your marketing materials and advertising.

You may not be able to have all these professionally printed until you make some money, but that never stopped me from using what I had available or could personally make up.

Remember, you can use your master-copy materials for any and all new clients you meet, so always have a few original sets ready to go. You will be working with more than one set of buyers at a time.

Once your Contracts of Purchase and Sale are prepared, you will spend triple or more time out meeting potential clients, and you can handle this added business without any problems at all. You are organized and ready for action.

I also had a number of the Ultimate Buyers' Presentation Packages set up. There are sections for information about you—including photographs, testimonials, references, awards and educational certificates—so you can select the items you want to include.

I know this sounds off the wall, but I also review everything about buyer's remorse with the Snerdles, so when they are ready to write, they know this could happen, but at least they are ready for it. No surprises. It will not stop them from making their offer. They are fully prepared for the negativity of what people could say that might scare them or cause concern.

You would be astounded at the number of my personal clients who called and thanked me for warning them about this. I hope you will do the same with all your clients.

By now, the Snerdles have happily accepted me as their agent, and your clients will do the same for you. In the first few days of working with the buyers, you most likely have not established enough rapport to specifically ask for referrals, but you do want to indicate that people like Mr. and Mrs. Happy referred you because they were satisfied, impressed and thrilled with your services. Introduce referrals early in the buying process.

Now, you'll move on to actually writing the contract. The agents who are already using my methods of preparing the Contract of Purchase and Sale and did download the material have indicated that they are now implementing the use of the 32 statements and the subjects that could be in most contracts when they initially begin their relationship with buyers.

Materials to Download

Below is a sample list of what is available to you on my website if you are interested, so please take a look. If this isn't the right time for you to take your career to the ultimate degree, then at least use the statements and subjects in this book, and prepare the most incredible Contracts of Purchase and Sale. You owe that to yourself, and I am disclosing and revealing the easiest, most comprehensive way of preparing your contracts.

This is step one in planning for a successful and profitable career, so it is a huge move in the right direction. You can access the website at www.barbarabellolsen.com when the timing is right for you.

Everything below is in word-processing documents for you to cut, copy, paste and edit to your preferences.

Forms—Over 200 pages of word-processing documents, including:

- Material Latent Defects | Disclosure

- Buyers' Must Haves and Would Like

- Confidentiality Agreement

- Consent/Permission to Disclose Personal Information Prospect Information

- Strata | Consent to Brokerage/Agents to Distribute Strata Council's Documents

- Thank You for Your Offer or Counter-Offer

- Why You Should Work With Me | I Am Your Professional Consultant and Advisor (Buyers' Copy)

Checklists:

- Arriving at the First Meeting with the Buyers Up and Until They Want to Write an Offer

- Questionnaire to Listing Agents/Reps | Prior to Writing an Offer

- Questionnaire to Listing Agents/Reps | Ready to Write an Offer

- Preparing a Contract | With Explanations

- Preparing a Contract | Without Explanations

- Presenting a Contract | With Explanations

- Presenting a Contract | Without Explanations

- Including Changing the Contract Prior to Subject Removal

- Including Subjects Removed/Fulfilled or Waived | Explanation

- After-Sale Service | After a Firm Sale | With Explanations

- After-Sale Service | After a Firm Sale | Without Explanations

Miscellaneous:

- Thank-You Notes and General Notes Samples

- Back-Up Offers | Items to Think of General Information

- To Do | For You!

- Sample Shopping List and Added Shopping List with Explanations

Full Possible Index:

- For Cover Sheets

- For Buyers' Presentation Packages or File Folder Headings or Labels

Financing:

- Finalization of the Preapproved Mortgage

- Satisfactory Financing

- Specific Details

- Can the Sellers Clear the Title?

Fire Property Insurance:

- Residential

- Strata

Inspection of the Property:

- Residential

- Strata

Property Specifics:

- Examples of What You May Add to a Contract

- Explanation and Information

- Sample Addendums

- Inspections | Right of Reinspection/Viewing

- Buyers Pay More than the Asking Price

- Unauthorized Accommodation

- Non-Conforming Use/Zoning/Code

- Non-Conforming Use Disclosed and Is Specifically Added in that the Sellers Have Disclosed All Material Latent Defects

Counter-Offer:

- Sample Regarding Dates and Times

- Sample Addendum | Changing the Dates after Acceptance of the Contract

- Amendment | Not Altering the Contract of Purchase and Sale

- Subject Removal

Clauses and Phrases—Over 700 pages, including statements, subjects, property-specific statements and subjects, again all in word-processing documents—just cut, copy and paste. I have done these in a few different ways for you:

- Just the clause by itself, ready to edit, copy and paste to your own documents

- On an addendum already pretyped

- On addendums for predisclosure, meaning you would use them when showing buyers properties and reviewing what may possibly end up in the contract when they are ready to make an offer.

The Ultimate Buyers' Presentation Package:

- Sample

- My Master File

All of my experience, advice and knowledge is available and ready to own and use right now on my website at   **www.barbarabellolsen.com**
Or e-mail me anytime at **barbarabellolsen@shaw.ca**

APPENDIX

AMENDMENT | DATE CHANGES | STATEMENT
[This is where it must be agreed to according to your buyers or they won't remove subjects]

SCHEDULE _____   MLS® #:   DATE   Page of
ADDRESS:
LEGAL:
PID:
Further to the Contract of Purchase and Sale Dated
Made Between   as buyers, and
                                                                        as sellers and
covering the above mentioned property. The undersigned hereby agree as follows

Statement
Changing the dates after Acceptance of the Contract of Purchase and Sale
For good and valuable consideration of *[One Dollar $1.00 or $_____]* given by the buyers and
hereby acknowledged and received by the sellers, the sellers and buyers mutually agree that the
Completion Date of *[state Date]* will now be *[state Date]*
Possession Date of *[state Date]* will now be *[state Date]*
Adjustment Date of *[state Date]* will now be *[state Date]*.
Time shall remain of the essence.
All other terms and conditions remain the same and in full force and effect.
[Do you want to add this in?]
This amendment is open for acceptance by the *[sellers/buyers]* until [Date and time].

All parties have been afforded the opportunity and advised to SEEK INDEPENDENT LEGAL/PROFESSIONAL ADVICE before signing this
Agreement. Time shall remain of the essence. All other terms and conditions remain the same and in full force and effect.
Signed, Sealed and Delivered in the Presence of   **In Witness Whereof I have hereunder set my hand and seal**

_____   _____   SEAL   _____

Witness   Buyer's Signature   Print Buyer's Name

_____   _____   SEAL   _____

Witness   Buyer's Signature   Print Buyer's Name

_____   _____   SEAL   _____

Witness   Seller's Signature   Print Seller's Name

_____   _____   SEAL   _____

Witness   Seller's Signature   Print Seller's Name

AMENDMENT | NOT ALTERING THE CONTRACT OF PURCHASE AND SALE
[This is where it does not have to be agreed to | the party requesting this will still remove their subjects and/or complete]

SCHEDULE _____   MLS® #:   DATE   Page of
ADDRESS:
LEGAL:
PID:
Further to the Contract of Purchase and Sale Dated
Made Between   as buyers, and
                                                                        as sellers and
covering the above mentioned property. The undersigned hereby agree as follows
In consideration for a payment to be made of $1.00 [One Dollar] and other good and valuable consideration, the *[sellers/buyers]* hereby request the *[sellers/buyers]* agreement to modify the terms of the Contract of Purchase and Sale as follows:
1.
2.
3.
[Do you want to add this in?]
This amendment is open for acceptance by the *[sellers/buyers]* until *[Date and time].*

In making this request, the *[sellers/buyers]* do not in any way repudiate or decline to honour any of the terms or conditions of the Contract of Purchase and Sale, and the *[sellers/buyers]* are free to decline this request if they wish, in which case the terms and conditions of the Contract of Purchase and Sale will remain binding on the parties without change.

If the *[sellers/buyers]* are willing to agree to modify the terms of the Contract of Purchase and Sale as set out herein, then by the parties signing this Amendment in the spaces provided below they hereby agree to modify the Contract of Purchase and Sale as set out above, and do further agree that:

1.   Time remains of the essence;

2.   The party to whom the consideration recited above is payable acknowledges having received such consideration; and

3.   The terms and conditions of the Contract of Purchase and Sale, except as specifically modified by this Addendum, remain in full force and effect.

All parties have been afforded the opportunity and advised to SEEK INDEPENDENT LEGAL/PROFESSIONAL ADVICE
before signing this Agreement.

Signed, Sealed and Delivered in the Presence of   **In Witness Whereof I have hereunder set my hand and seal**

Witness	Buyer's Signature	Print Buyer's Name
Witness	Buyer's Signature	Print Buyer's Name
Witness	Seller's Signature	Print Seller's Name
Witness	Seller's Signature	Print Seller's Name

Make sure the $1.00 is paid and attach the receipt

Barbara Bell-Olsen

CHECKLIST | FOR TURNING IN DOCUMENTS WITH YOUR SALES CONTRACT

Date the Following Items Were Given to the Administrator:_____

Full MLS® Printout

Government documentation

Buyer Agency Acknowledgement

"Working with a REALTOR® Brochure" properly executed [even if is in your listing file]

Property Disclosure Statement *signed* by all parties [even if is in your listing file]

Title Search [even if is in your listing file]

Business | Affidavit

Buyer Agency Contract

Cancellation |Release of Trust Funds & General Release

Confidentiality Agreement Forms

Confirm Your Advice [CYA] Form

Consent to Advertise Unauthorized Accommodation

Contract | Clearer copy if needed

Deposits | Bank draft/money order Date given to Office

         | Uncertified cheque | Please follow up that it clears

         | Wire Transfer – copy if initiation instructions from the Financial Institute

         | To receive Interest Yes   No   SIN # *[if applicable]*

Deposits | Declaration Acknowledgement Form

Deposits | Irrevocable Instructions to the Seller's Lawyer/Notary re the holding of

Disclosure | Delaying the presentation and/or showing times

Disclosure | Interest in Trade

Disclosure | Material Latent Defects [could be the CYA Form]

Disclosure | Presentation of Offers only by you

Disclosure | Reducing or increasing your Commission

Disclosure | Referral Fees/Benefits

Disclosure | Remuneration

Disclosure | Revocation Forms/documentation

Fee Agreements

Lawyer and/or Notary Information | Buyers and Sellers

Limited Dual Agency Agreement

Material Latent Defects | Disclosure of

Material Latent Defects | Information for Sellers Form

Measurements | Square footage/lot size/ etc. could be a Form

Signing authority | Proof of/Power of Attorney/Estate Sale/Court Ordered Sale/Relocation

Company/etc Signing authority | Written Instructions to Sign on behalf of your Clients

Strata | Form B   and F

Strata | Pertinent documents

Strata | "Disclosure of Benefits |Rental/Strata Property Management Services" Form

Tenancy |Mutual Agreement to End the Tenancy or signed agreement

Tenancy | Notice asking the Tenants to vacate

Tenancy | Rental Agreements

Tenancy | Termination Letters

Any other pertinent documents

CONFIDENTIALITY AGREEMENT

Re Property _____

| Address | City | Province | Postal Code |

Legal_____PID #_____

Name of Sellers_____

Name of Sellers_____

| Phone Numbers | Address | City | Province | Postal Code |

Name of Buyers_____

Name of Buyers_____

| Phone Numbers | Address | City | Province | Postal Code |

Listing Agents/Reps _____

Agents and Contact Info

Listing Brokerage_____

Brokerage name and Contact Info

Buyers Agents/Reps _____

Agents and Contact Info

Buyers Brokerage _____

Brokerage name and Contact Info

All the parties above agree that any price, counter price, offers, terms and/or conditions, financial information disclosed or received and information in any offers on the above named property address will not be discussed or disclosed to any other Buyers or potential Buyers or any other parties including other Agents/REALTORS® and/or Brokerages without the prior written consent of the Sellers and Buyers.

All parties have been afforded the opportunity and advised to
SEEK INDEPENDENT LEGAL/PROFESSIONAL ADVICE before signing this Confidentiality Agreement

In Witness Whereof I have hereunder set my hand and seal Signed, Sealed and Delivered in the Presence of

_____
Seller's Signature   Witness   Date

_____
Seller's Signature   Witness   Date

_____
Buyer's Signature   Witness   Date

_____
Buyer's Signature   Witness   Date

_____
Seller's Agent's Signature Witness   Date

_____
Buyer's Agent's Signature Witness   Date

Receipt of this Confidentiality Agreement should be cross-referenced in the Contract of Purchase and Sale
Your Authorities/Legislators may have a prescribed form you must use

Barbara Bell-Olsen

CONFIRM YOUR ADVICE *[CYA]*

Waiver of Including Statements/Subjects [Condition Precedents] in the Contract of Purchase and Sale
The Buyers acknowledge as indicated by their signatures below that they have been advised by
Agents/Representatives _____ of Brokerage _____
that it is common practice to include the following statements/subjects in their Contract of Purchase and
Sale for the property located at _____

| [Address] | [City] | [Province] |

Legal Description _____ [PID}_____
prior to entering into the Contract of Purchase and Sale and the Buyers have chosen to waive those they
have signed & acknowledged below. They have been **advised and afforded the opportunity to obtain
INDEPENDENT LEGAL/PROFESSIONAL ADVICE** including but not limited to Financial Institutes Appraisers/
Insurance/Inspectors/Surveyors/Environmental issues and any City/Municipal/Regional/Governmental
Authorities, including if applicable the Strata Property Management Company, the Strata Manager/ Council
etc. regarding any and all possible ramifications of not including such protective statements/ subjects. The
Buyers are fully aware of any and all ramifications and any/all consequences by not including these items for
their own protection and have chosen to proceed without the following subjects /concerns being specified
as evidenced by their signatures beside the recommended clause below -
BUYERS' ACKNOWLEDGEMENT AND WAIVER BY SIGNATURES [BESIDE ITEMS THEY DO NOT WANT INCLUDED IN THE CONTRACT]
_____ Subject to financing [mortgaging] and/or appraisal
_____ Subject to fire/property insurance
_____ Subject to the Property Disclosure Statement
_____ Subject to the Title Search including easements/restrictive covenants and
non-financial charges that will remain on Title
_____ Subject to a professional inspection of the Property
_____ Subject to oil tank/septic or other environmental inspection
_____ Subject to Legal/Professional or other advice
_____ Subject to obtaining Title Insurance
_____ Subject to _____
_____ Subject to _____
_____ Subject to the Strata Corporations rules and regulations, current budget and
the Developer's Rental Disclosure Statement, Depreciation Report
_____ Subject to the registered strata plan, any amendments to the strata plan, and
any resolutions dealing with changes to common property;
_____ Subject to the current by-laws and financial statements of the strata
corporation, and any section to which the strata corporation lot belongs;
_____ Subject to the minutes of any meeting by the strata council, and by the
members in annual, extraordinary or special general meetings, and by the
members or the executive of any section to which the strata lot belongs.
_____ Subject to any and all Engineering/Remediation/ correspondence/ reports/
studies, Envelope correspondence/reports/studies, any Legal correspondence/
opinions/documents and any/all warranty and insurance claims/
correspondence/documents/information
_____ Subject to the designation/use/location of the parking stall[s] and locker[s]
_____ Subject to the Strata Insurance Policy
The Buyers' Agents/Representatives/Brokerage have advised the Buyers that it is proper practice to include the above items [if
applicable] & receive & review any/all documents & that the Buyers have declined to do so & are aware of any ramifications that
could occur. **In Witness Whereof I have hereunder set my hand and seal Signed, Sealed and Delivered in the Presence of**

_____
Buyer's Signature & Acknowledgement   Witness   Date

_____
Buyer's Signature & Acknowledgement   Witness   Date

Your Authorities/Legislators may have a prescribed form you must use

DISCLAIMERS | SAMPLES

*This message and any attachments are intended for the designated recipients only and may contain privileged, confidential or copyrighted information under applicable law. If you have received it in error, please notify the sender immediately and double delete it from your 'inbox' and 'deleted folders.'

This communication is for use by the intended recipient and contains information that is privileged, confidential or copyrighted under applicable law. If you are not the intended recipient, you are hereby formally notified that any use, copying or distribution of any of this information in whole or part, is strictly prohibited. Please notify the sender by return e-mail and delete this e-mail and any attachments from the system.

This e-mail and any attachments may contain information that is privileged and/or confidential. If you are not the intended recipient and appear to have received this e-mail in error, please notify us immediately and then delete all copies from your computer system. Any unauthorized use, copying or further distribution is prohibited.

This message [and attachments if included] is confidential and is not be forwarded to any third party without express written consent of the sender. If you have received this message in error please notify the sender and double-delete the message from your Inbox and Deleted Items folders.

E-Mails and Confirming If the Information Being Sent Is a Contract

This was from a couple of lawyers who were negotiating back and forth and no signatures were ever obtained according to the article in the paper but it was upheld by a Court so they suggested we should consider using this depending on the circumstances.

"E-mails sent or received shall neither constitute acceptance of conducting transactions via electronic means nor shall create a binding contract in the absence of a fully signed written contract."

The Following Clauses Must Appear on Any Solicitations You Send Out Including E-Mails

This communication is not intended to cause or induce breach of an existing Listing Brokerage Agreement or Buyer Agency Contract.

Under the Privacy Act You Should Include an Opt-Out Clause on All Mailings/E-Mails/Etc. (Example Shown Below)

In our endeavours to provide information to past and current clients, we regularly send real estate related information such as this. However, should you not wish to receive future mailings, please let me know and I will remove your name from my database. [Include your Brokerage, your name and how they can reach you.]

Website | Alert

You must include the full name of your employing Brokerage on each and every page of your website. It must be the full name. Please check your Rules and Regulations and make sure you are in compliance.

Advertising / Newspapers

Also, when advertising in the newspaper, etc., you must always include your employing Brokerage name in full | no shortcuts.

Barbara Bell-Olsen

INSPECTION REPORTS | PERMISSION TO DISTRIBUTE THE INSPECTION REPORT

RE PROPERTY ADDRESS _____

              Address   City   Province   Postal Code

Legal_____ PID #_____

TO _____

_____

Phone Numbers   Address   City   Province   Postal Code

_____

This is to authorize that you and any of your Agents/Reps/Brokerages may distribute the attached Inspection Report to prospective *[Sellers/Buyers]* or their Agents/Reps/Brokerages. It may also be given to the *[Sellers/Buyers]* and their Agents/Reps/Brokerages.

Comments | Notes _____

_____

_____

FROM _____

_____

Phone Numbers   Address   City   Province   Postal Code

_____

**All parties have been afforded the opportunity and advised to
SEEK INDEPENDENT LEGAL/PROFESSIONAL ADVICE before signing this Confidentiality Agreement**

In Witness Whereof I have hereunder set my hand and seal Signed, Sealed and Delivered in the Presence of

_____
Inspector's Signing Authority   Witness   Date

_____
Inspector's Signing Authority   Witness   Date

_____
[Seller's/Buyer's] Authority   Witness   Date

_____
[Seller's/Buyer's] Authority   Witness   Date

Your Authorities/Legislators may have a prescribed form you must use

INSPECTIONS | RIGHT OF REINSPECTION/VIEWING | STATEMENT | ADDENDUM

SCHEDULE _____   MLS® #:   DATE   Page of

ADDRESS:

LEGAL:

PID:

Further to the Contract of Purchase and Sale Dated

Made Between   as Buyers, and

                                           as Sellers and

covering the above mentioned property. The undersigned hereby agree as follows

Statement
Inspections | Right of Reinspection/Viewing

The Sellers and Buyers mutually agree that the Sellers shall have the right to reinspect/view the land/property/buildings/structures *[one/two]* further times at a mutually agreed upon time provided that *[24 hour]* *[written]* notice is given from the Buyers to the Sellers. The maximum time the Buyers are allowed for the agreed visits is *[2 hours]*. The Buyers at the time of serving the written notice will specifically specify who will accompany them on the visits including but not limited to the Buyers/Buyers' Agents/Representatives/Brokerage/Architects/Interior Designers/Contractors and the like Professions for premeasuring/decorating/planning purposes. The Sellers warrant that this notice will not be unreasonably withheld.

The Sellers agree to allow access for any of these parties if required including those already agreed to in the Access for All Trades Statement.

All parties have been afforded the opportunity and advised to SEEK INDEPENDENT LEGAL/PROFESSIONAL ADVICE before signing this Agreement. Time shall remain of the essence. All other terms and conditions remain the same and in full force and effect.

Signed, Sealed and Delivered in the Presence of   **In Witness Whereof I have hereunder set my hand and seal**

_____   _____ (SEAL) _____

Witness   Buyer's Signature   Print Buyer's Name

_____   _____ (SEAL) _____

Witness   Buyer's Signature   Print Buyer's Name

_____   _____ (SEAL) _____

Witness   Seller's Signature   Print Seller's Name

_____   _____   _____

Witness   Seller's Signature   Print Seller's Name

MATERIAL LATENT DEFECTS | DISCLOSURE

Property Address_____ ["The Property"]

Legal _____PID _____

To be in compliance with the requirements of the Legislation, the Sellers and Buyers hereby acknowledge that full disclosure of any material latent defects was made prior to entering into a Contract of Purchase and Sale.

☐ "The Property" as legally described above **HAS** the following Material Latent Defects

_____
_____
_____

☐ To the best of the Sellers' knowledge, the Sellers warrant and guarantee that there are <u>NO FURTHER</u> material latent defects other than those disclosed above. _____ Initials

☐ To the best of the Sellers' knowledge, the Sellers warrant and guarantee that there are <u>NO</u> material latent defects. _____Initials

The parties have also been advised and afforded the opportunity to do their own investigation with any City/Municipal/Regional/Governmental/Environmental Authorities/Legal/Professional Advisors regarding lack of permits, unauthorized accommodation, renovations without permits, underground oil tanks or any other concerns they may have. The Sellers consent and agree to the predistribution of this Disclosure to any prospective/interested Buyers/Real Estate Agents/Reps/Brokerages including via electronic means.

All parties to this Disclosure have been afforded the opportunity and advised to SEEK INDEPENDENT LEGAL/PROFESSIONAL ADVICE and been advised to confirm and/or research all Disclosures made prior to entering into a Contract of Purchase and Sale as evidenced by their signatures and the disclosure dates below.

	In Witness Whereof I have hereunder set my hand and seal	Signed, Sealed and Delivered in the Presence of

SEAL _____   _____
    Print Name   Signature of the Sellers   Witness

Date: *Prior to entering into a Contract of Purchase and Sale* _____20__

SEAL _____   _____
    Print Name   Signature of the Sellers   Witness

Date: *Prior to entering into a Contract of Purchase and Sale* _____20__

SEAL _____   _____
    Print Name   Signature of the Buyers   Witness

Date: *Prior to entering into a Contract of Purchase and Sale* _____20__

SEAL _____   _____
    Print Name   Signature of the Buyers   Witness

Date: *Prior to entering into a Contract of Purchase and Sale* _____20__

Your Authorities/Legislators may have a prescribed form you must use

MEASUREMENTS, SQUARE FOOTAGE, LOT SIZE [IF APPLICABLE], AGE INFORMATION & DISCLOSURE

Date _____

Re _____

[Unit Number if applicable] and Property Address

City _____ Province _____ Postal Code _____

Legal: _____ PID #_____

This information and disclosure is made

To_____

Name of Parties to whom this disclosure and information is being given to – usually the Buyers and possibly their Agents/Representative

1. The following indicates how the undersigned Agents/Reps/Brokerage obtained the age of the buildings. Further information can be obtained from Government/Municipal/Regional Authorities. _____

The following indicates how the undersigned Agents/Reps/Brokerage obtained the measurements, square footage and/or lot size [If applicable] _____

2. Agents/Reps Measurements - room sizes, square footage and/or lot size if applicable - Date_____

Comments_____

_____

_____

_____

3. Other Source of Measurements - room sizes, square footage and/or lot size if applicable -

Date_____

Comments_____

_____

_____

_____

_____

[Attach a second page if necessary and any other applicable documentation]

The Buyers have been advised that if further information or exact measurements, square footage and/or lot size is a concern, the property should be independently measured and the Buyers should make their own investigations as to the age of the buildings. The Buyers are advised to verify the above information and arrange for any independent measurements and/or investigation at the earliest possible convenience and in any event prior to proceeding with the Contract. The Buyers have been advised to make this a subject for their sole benefit in the Contract of Purchase and Sale.

Disclosed by Agents/Reps Names and Signatures   Brokerage   Witness   Date

All parties have been afforded the opportunity and advised to
SEEK INDEPENDENT LEGAL/PROFESSIONAL ADVICE before signing this Agreement

"The parties" to this Disclosure accept and acknowledge the above information and have put a subject in the Contract of Purchase and Sale. [Signatures] Yes_____ No_____

"The parties" to this Disclosure accept and acknowledge the above information and have waived their right to put a subject in the Contract of Purchase and Sale and are satisfied with the information as provided. [Signatures] Yes_____ No_____

In Witness Whereof I have hereunder set my hand and seal Signed, Sealed and Delivered in the Presence of Date

SEAL _____

Buyer's Signature   Witness   Day   Month   Year

SEAL _____

Buyer's Signature   Witness   Day   Month   Year

Your Authorities/Legislators may have a prescribed form you must use

MORTGAGE VERIFICATION | CONFIDENTIAL

LENDER [the "Lender"]
TO:_____

        Name of Lender [the "Lender"]

Address	City	Province	Postal Code

Area Code/Phone	Fax	E-mail

BORROWER [the "Borrower"]
RE:_____

        Name of Borrowers [the "Borrower"]

Home Address	City	Province	Postal Code

Area Code/Phone	Fax	E-mail

Mortgaged Property:_____

Address	City	Province	Postal Code

Legal _____PID _____

Mortgage Account Number:_____

BROKERAGE [the "Agent"]

Name of Agents/Reps	Name of Brokerage

Address	City	Province	Postal Code

Area Code/Phone	Fax	E-mail

I hereby authorize the "Lender" to furnish the mortgage information below to my "Agent"

_____

[Month/Day/Year]	Sellers' Signatures

MORTGAGE INFORMATION [To be completed by the "Lender"]

Lenders: _____

Date of Mortgage:_____ Original Principal Amount $_____

Interest Rate_____ Term_____ Amortization_____

Date of Maturity:_____Current Principal Balance $_____

Monthly Payment: Principal and Interest $_____ Taxes $_____

Total Monthly Payment $_____ Next payment date [Month/Day/Year]_____

Lien Position: 1st Mortgage_____2nd Mortgage_____Other_____ Are Payments Current?_____

If No, amount in arrears $_____ & periods of arrears_____Is the mortgage assumable?_____

Assumable with qualification ___ Assumable without qualification ___Assumption fee if any $_____

Termination fee or prepayment penalty if any Yes _____No _____$_____

ADDITIONAL INFORMATION WHICH MAY BE OF ASSISTANCE_____

_____

_____

Signatures on behalf of the "Lender"	Titles	[Month/Day/Year]

Your Authorities/Legislators may have a prescribed form you must use

OVER ASKING PRICE STATEMENT | ADDENDUM

SCHEDULE _____   MLS® #:   DATE   Page of

ADDRESS:

LEGAL:

PID:

Further to the Contract of Purchase and Sale Dated

Made Between   as Buyers, and

                                                               as Sellers and

covering the above mentioned property. The undersigned hereby agree as follows

Statement

Over Asking Price | Buyers pay more than the Asking Price

The Buyers are aware that the amount of this offer to purchase is in excess of the listing price or advertised price for this property and waive any rights to subsequent recovery of such higher amount.

All parties have been afforded the opportunity and advised to SEEK INDEPENDENT LEGAL/PROFESSIONAL ADVICE before signing this Agreement. Time shall remain of the essence. All other terms and conditions remain the same and in full force and effect.

Signed, Sealed and Delivered in the Presence of   **In Witness Whereof I have hereunder set my hand and seal**

_____   _____ (SEAL) _____

Witness   Buyer's Signature   Print Buyer's Name

_____   _____ (SEAL) _____

Witness   Buyer's Signature   Print Buyer's Name

_____   _____ (SEAL) _____

Witness   Seller's Signature   Print Seller's Name

_____   _____ (SEAL) _____

Witness   Seller's Signature   Print Seller's Name

Barbara Bell-Olsen

PRESENTATION OF OFFERS | DELAYED TO A SPECIFIC DATE AND/OR TIME
[Any colleagues inquiring on this property | send them a copy of these instructions immediately]

We _____
Name of Sellers

Owners of _____
Property Address

Legal _____ PID _____

Authorize our Agents/Reps _____
Names and Contact Info

Of_____
Brokerage name

_____
Address   City   Province   Postal Code   Phone Number

that we will not be prepared to review any offers on our above property until

_____ _____ 20_____ at _____
Day   Month   Year   Time

This is your written authorization to advise your fellow Agents/Reps/Brokerages and Prospects/ Clients/ Customers that we will only review offers as stated above. You have fully informed us of both the pros and cons of this stipulation.
All parties have been afforded the opportunity and advised to
SEEK INDEPENDENT LEGAL/PROFESSIONAL ADVICE before signing this Agreement
In Witness Whereof I have hereunder set my hand and seal   **Signed, Sealed and Delivered in the Presence of**

SEAL _____   _____
Seller's Signature   Witness

Date_____

SEAL _____   _____
Seller's Signature   Witness

Date_____

SEAL _____   _____
Seller's Signature   Witness

Date_____

SEAL _____   _____
Seller's Signature   Witness

Date_____
Your Authorities/Legislators may have a prescribed form you must use

PRESENTATION OF OFFERS | DIRECTION THAT ONLY
THE LISTING AGENTS TO PRESENT OFFERS

[Any colleagues inquiring on this property | send them a copy of these instructions immediately]

We _____

Name of Sellers

Owners of _____

Property Address

Legal _____ PID _____

Authorize our Agents/Reps _____

Names and Contact Info

And Brokerage _____

| Address | City | Province | Postal Code | Phone Number |

to personally receive and present any and all relevant information and offers that are received on our property.

If we require any further information regarding any offers we shall advise our Agents/Reps.

Thank you in advance for your understanding and co-operation.

| **In Witness Whereof I have hereunder set my hand and seal** | **Signed, Sealed and Delivered in the Presence of** |

(SEAL) _____
Seller's Signature

_____
Witness

Date_____

(SEAL) _____
Seller's Signature

_____
Witness

Date_____

(SEAL) _____
Seller's Signature

_____
Witness

Date_____

(SEAL) _____
Seller's Signature

_____
Witness

Date_____

Your Authorities/Legislators may have a prescribed form you must use

QUESTIONNAIRE TO LISTING AGENTS/REPS | *PRIOR TO* WRITING AN OFFER
Page 1 of 2

My buyers seem very interested, and if we write an offer I am hoping you could help me with anything special that your sellers might require.

Is the property still available, and you are co-operating?

Have you had any offers?

Are you expecting any offers?

If you do get any offers or think any offers are coming in, would you please call me and let me know?

Any particular reason they are selling?

Have they bought or do they need to buy?

Do the sellers have any preference regarding completion, possession and adjustment dates?

Any items the sellers want to take with them? (Confirm the included and excluded items.)

Could you please e-mail/fax/text me a copy of the Title Search and the completed Property Disclosure Statement? (Give the agent your e-mail/fax number and confirm it in writing when this conversation is over.)

Any disclosures that my buyers might need to know about?

Do you know if there is an oil tank?

Are any of the sellers real estate agents, or are the agents/reps related to the sellers? Do they have any business interest requiring disclosure to the buyers?

Is the seller a resident of [_____]? (If there are two or more sellers, ask if both or all the sellers are residents of [_____]. Make sure you ask this question.)

Could you please also e-mail/fax/text me proof of signing authority for the sellers? (Ask this if the title shows in another name or business, etc.)

Anything else I should include in the offer?

Is there anything else you could advise that would help your sellers?

If my people do write, I will contact you immediately, but is there a special time or day that you could present the offer?

Are your sellers easy to see to present an offer?

QUESTIONNAIRE TO LISTING AGENTS/REPS | *PRIOR TO* WRITING AN OFFER
Page 2 of 2

How long should I leave the acceptance date and time open for?

My buyers have asked if I will present their offer in person. Is that okay with you and your sellers?

Will you please keep my name and contact information on file, and if anything progresses on the property, please give me a call?

(Thank the agent for all the helpful information and say you look forward to working together.)

(Send an e-mail/fax/text thanking the listing representative and providing all your contact information so you can be contacted if something happens between now and the time you present your offer. Remind the agent to send you the documents you asked for: the Property Disclosure Statement, the Title Search, disclosures and stigmas if applicable, and any other documents/statements and instructions.)

QUESTIONNAIRE TO LISTING AGENTS/REPS | *READY TO* WRITE AN OFFER
Page 1 of 2

My buyers seem very interested, and if we write an offer I am hoping you could help me with anything special that your sellers might require.

Is the property still available and obviously you are co-operating? Thanks.

Have you had any offers?

Are you expecting any offers?

If you do get any offers or think any offers are coming in, would you please call me and let me know?

Any particular reason they are selling?

Have they bought or do they need to buy?

Do the sellers have any preference regarding completion, possession and adjustment dates?

Any items the sellers want to take with them? (Confirm the included and excluded items.)

Could you please e-mail/fax/text me a copy of the Title Search and the completed Property Disclosure Statement? (Hopefully you already have this.)

Are there any unexplainable restrictive covenants or easements? If so, could you also please send a copy of the full explanation? (Give the agent your e-mail/fax number and confirm it in writing when the conversation is over.)

Any disclosures that my buyers might need to know about? Do you know if there is an oil tank, septic tank or any other item?

Are there any tenancies? (If so, ask for all the tenancy information and copies of any rent documents/leases, etc. Is it unauthorized accommodation and therefore possibly a material latent defect?)

Are any of the sellers real estate agents, or are the agents/reps related to the sellers? Do they have any business interest requiring disclosure to the buyers?

Is the seller a resident of [_____] as per the Income Tax Act? (If there are two or more sellers, please ask if both or all the sellers are residents of [_____]. Make sure you ask this question.)

Could you please also e-mail/fax/text me proof of signing authority for the sellers? (Ask this if the title shows in another name or business, etc.)

Anything else I should include in the offer?

QUESTIONNAIRE TO LISTING AGENTS/REPS | *READY TO* WRITE AN OFFER
Page 2 of 2

Is there anything else you could advise that would help your Sellers?

If my people do write, I will contact you immediately, but is there a special time or day that you could present the offer?

Are your sellers easy to see to present an offer?

How long should I leave the acceptance date and time open for?

My buyers have asked if I will present their offer in person. Is that okay with you and your sellers?

Will you please keep my name and contact information on file, and if anything progresses on the property please give me a call?

(Thank the agent for all the helpful information and say you look forward to working together.)

(Send an e-mail/fax/text thanking the listing representative and providing all your contact information so you can be contacted if something happens between now and the time you present your offer. Remind the agent to send you the documents you asked for: the Property Disclosure Statement, the Title Search, disclosures and stigmas if applicable, and any other documents/statements and instructions.)

Barbara Bell-Olsen

SIGNING ON BEHALF OF YOUR CLIENTS/CUSTOMERS
LETTER OF AUTHORITY TO SIGN ON BEHALF OF YOUR CLIENTS/CUSTOMERS

We the undersigned hereby authorize _____
Agents/Reps

Of _____ to act as our Agents/Reps and sign
Brokerage/Address/Contact Info

On our behalf any documents for the _____ of the property known as
Purchase/Sale

_____
Address/City/Province/Postal

And legally described as _____

PID # _____

And we confirm the terms and conditions are as follows:

1. Deposit $ _____
    By Bank Draft or Money Order upon acceptance of this Contract by all parties or upon removal of all subjects or_____
2. Price $ _____
3. Subject to financing or _____
4. *All subjects are for the sole benefit of the Buyers or_____*
5. Subjects to be removed in writing by Date _____
6. Enter all other subjects/terms, [e.g. deposit increases, repairs to be undertaken, etc.] _____
7. Completion date is _____ 20 _____
8. Possession date is _____ 20 _____
9. Adjustment date is _____ 20 _____
10. Purchase price to include _____
11. *Time shall remain of the essence. All other terms and conditions as per the form of the Contract of Purchase and Sale or remain the same and in full force and effect*

**All parties have been afforded the opportunity and advised to
SEEK INDEPENDENT LEGAL/PROFESSIONAL ADVICE before signing this Agreement**

We hereby authorize and direct you as our Agents/Reps to sign and initial where necessary, the Contract of Purchase and Sale/addendums/amendments and subsequent subject removal documents on our behalf in accordance with the above written terms and conditions.

_____   _____
Print full Legal Name of Sellers/Buyers giving Authorization   Date

_____   _____
Signature of Sellers/Buyers giving Authorization   Witness

Date: *prior to signing any Documents* _____ 20__

_____   _____
Print full Legal Name of Sellers/Buyers giving Authorization   Date

_____   _____
Signature of Sellers/Buyers giving Authorization   Witness

Date: *prior to signing any Documents* _____ 20__

Your Authorities/Legislators may have a prescribed form you must use

STATEMENTS IN MOST CONTRACTS | INDEX

1. Legal/Professional Advice | Standard Care
2. Acceptance of All Statements
3. Access for All Trades
4. Appliances—Buyers' Acceptance Of
5. Furniture or Other Items/Equipment Being Sold By Sellers
6. Rental or Leased Agreements/Contracts
7. Confidentiality Agreement
8. Deposits | Legal Advice
9. Deposits—If Any Interest Is Accrued
10. Incorporation of Documents
11. Measurements/Room Sizes/Square Footage/Lot Size/Age
12. No Growth or Manufacture of Illegal Substances
13. Outstanding Orders
14. Plans/Permits/Documents/Drawings Will Be Supplied by the Sellers
15. Property Disclosure
16. Referral Fee Disclosure
17. Remuneration Disclosure
18. Registering In another Name *[Do Not Use and/or Nominee]*
19. Residents
20. Returning of the Sellers' Documents
21. Sellers Agree To Allow Time for Buyers to Remove Subjects
22. Sellers Have Disclosed Material Latent Defects
23. Sellers Hereby Authorize Buyers to Obtain Documents and Information [This Puts the Buyers in the Sellers' Shoes]
24. Sellers Will Sign Necessary Documentation and Allow Access
25. Separate Disclosures | Statements
26. Survey
27. Taxes | Accounting/Professional Advice
28. Taxes | Property Assessments
29. Taxes | Property Transfer Tax Statement
30. Title Insurance
31. Title Search
32. Waiver of Subjects

STATEMENTS | ADDENDUM | LEGAL/PROFESSIONAL ADVICE | STANDARD CARE
AND ACCEPTANCE OF ALL STATEMENTS [32]

SCHEDULE _____   MLS® #:   DATE   Page of
ADDRESS:
LEGAL:
PID:
Further to the Contract of Purchase and Sale Dated
Made Between   as Buyers, and
                                                         as Sellers and
covering the above mentioned property. The undersigned hereby agree as follows

LEGAL/PROFESSIONAL ADVICE | STANDARD CARE
*The *[Sellers/Buyers or the Sellers and Buyers]* acknowledge that the Agents/Representatives/Brokerages providing agency services to the Sellers and Buyers do not provide Legal/Professional/Accounting/ Construction/Engineering/Environmental/Tax/Zoning or other expert advice in matters beyond the common standard of care in the Real Estate Industry. The parties have been *[afforded the opportunity and]* advised to seek independent or other expert advice *[and waived their right to do so]* prior to entering into this Contract of Purchase and Sale *[and warrant and guarantee that they shall hold harmless and indemnify the Sellers' and Buyers' Agents/Representatives/Brokerages from any claims, actions or causes of action that may be the result of any and all issues or uses of the land/property/buildings/structures]*.

ACCEPTANCE OF ALL STATEMENTS
*The *[Sellers/Buyers or the Sellers and Buyers]* have been advised prior to entering into this Contract of Purchase and Sale that if any of the Statements/wording in this Contract of Purchase and Sale are a concern or they want further explanation/clarification they must make them a subject to their investigation/ research and not remain as accepted and acknowledged statements. The *[Sellers/Buyers or the Sellers and Buyers]* confirm they are in agreement with any and all Statements/wording as written and are aware of any possible ramification of this legal, binding and enforceable Contract of Purchase and Sale.

This Schedule is hereby incorporated and forms part of this Contract of Purchase and Sale entered into by the parties as evidenced by their signatures below.

All parties have been afforded the opportunity and advised to SEEK INDEPENDENT LEGAL/PROFESSIONAL ADVICE before signing this Agreement. Time shall remain of the essence. All other terms and conditions remain the same and in full force and effect.

Signed, Sealed and Delivered in the Presence of   **In Witness Whereof I have hereunder set my hand and seal**

_____   _____   (SEAL)   _____
Witness   Buyer's Signature   Print Buyer's Name

_____   _____   (SEAL)   _____
Witness   Buyer's Signature   Print Buyer's Name

_____   _____   (SEAL)   _____
Witness   Seller's Signature   Print Seller's Name

_____   _____   (SEAL)   _____
Witness   Seller's Signature   Print Seller's Name

STATEMENTS | ADDENDUM | ACCESS FOR ALL TRADES

SCHEDULE _____ MLS® #:   DATE   Page of
ADDRESS:
LEGAL:
PID:
Further to the Contract of Purchase and Sale Dated
Made Between   as Buyers, and
                                                       as Sellers and
covering the above mentioned property. The undersigned hereby agree as follows

ACCESS FOR ALL TRADES
*The Sellers, at no cost to the Sellers, *[unless otherwise mutually agreed to in writing]* warrant and
guarantee to allow access to the land/property/buildings/structures by any of the trades for their
purpose on reasonable *[or 24 hours]* *[written]* notice, including but not limited to Appraisers, Engineers,
Environmentalists, Financiers, Inspectors, Insurers, Surveyors or other Professional Agents/Representatives
of the Buyers' choice.
OR
The Sellers consent and will allow access to the property by any of the 'trades' for their purpose
on reasonable notice, including but not limited to financiers, appraisers, insurers, surveyors and
inspectors.*[You may want to insert a time frame they are allowed in.]

It is mutually agreed and confirmed that the Buyers/Buyers' Agents or Representatives may accompany the
trades when they access.

You may want to insert a time frame | e.g. within [___calendar] days of acceptance of this Contract of
Purchase and Sale by all parties or [an actual date – e.g. 3 days before the subject removal date – e.g. 3 days
before all subject removals is September 15th therefore use September 12th as the date] and in some cases it
may even be [completion date].

This Schedule is hereby incorporated and forms part of this Contract of Purchase and Sale entered into by
the parties as evidenced by their signatures below.
All parties have been afforded the opportunity and advised to SEEK INDEPENDENT LEGAL/PROFESSIONAL ADVICE before signing this
Agreement. Time shall remain of the essence. All other terms and conditions remain the same and in full force and effect.
Signed, Sealed and Delivered in the Presence of   In Witness Whereof I have hereunder set my hand and seal

_____   _____   _____
Witness   Buyer's Signature   Print Buyer's Name

_____   _____   _____
Witness   Buyer's Signature   Print Buyer's Name

_____   _____   _____
Witness   Seller's Signature   Print Seller's Name

_____   _____   _____
Witness   Seller's Signature   Print Seller's Name

STATEMENTS | ADDENDUM | APPLIANCES—BUYERS' ACCEPTANCE OF AND
FURNITURE OR OTHER ITEMS/EQUIPMENT BEING SOLD BY SELLERS

SCHEDULE _____ MLS® #:   DATE   Page of
ADDRESS:
LEGAL:
PID:
Further to the Contract of Purchase and Sale Dated
Made Between   as Buyers, and
                                                            as Sellers and
covering the above mentioned property. The undersigned hereby agree as follows

APPLIANCES—BUYERS' ACCEPTANCE OF
*The Buyers understand and acknowledge that the Sellers are not making any express or implied warranties/guarantees and that while the included items will be in substantially the same condition on possession date as when viewed, they are not new and as such are not guaranteed or warranted by the Sellers. The Sellers, at no cost to the Sellers, agree to provide appliance manuals, instruction manuals and warranty information applicable to any appliances/chattels/equipment/fixtures included in the purchase price, if available on or before possession date.

OR
*Within *[3 calendar]* days of acceptance of this Contract of Purchase and Sale by all Parties, the Sellers will provide a signed and dated list of the make/brand name, model, serial number and colour of all appliances included at no cost to the Buyers or the Buyers' Agents/Representatives/Brokerage; which will be incorporated into and form part of this contract. The Sellers, at no cost to the Sellers, agree to provide appliance manuals, instruction manuals and warranty information applicable to any appliances/chattels/equipment/fixtures included in the purchase price, if available.

FURNITURE OR OTHER ITEMS/EQUIPMENT BEING SOLD BY SELLERS
*The Sellers warrant and guarantee to give the Buyers the right of first refusal to negotiate for the purchase of any furniture or items/equipment to be sold by the Sellers upon a mutually agreed written price between the Sellers and Buyers. The parties are aware there may be a tax involved, applicable to the sale of such items and have been advised to confirm with their *[Accountant/Income Tax Department/ Legal or Professional Advisors or your Authorities/Regulators]* prior to entering into any separate written agreement. Should the Sellers and Buyers not come to a mutual agreement on or before *[date]* the Buyers' right of first refusal shall become null and void and the Sellers are able to negotiate or contract with others. This separate written purchase and sale for furniture or other items/equipment is for the benefit of the Sellers and Buyers and will be negotiated privately between the parties and not form part of this Contract of Purchase and Sale. Time shall remain of the essence.

This Schedule is hereby incorporated and forms part of this Contract of Purchase and Sale entered into by the parties as evidenced by their signatures below.
All parties have been afforded the opportunity and advised to SEEK INDEPENDENT LEGAL/PROFESSIONAL ADVICE before signing this Agreement. Time shall remain of the essence. All other terms and conditions remain the same and in full force and effect.
Signed, Sealed and Delivered in the Presence of   **In Witness Whereof I have hereunder set my hand and seal**

_____   _____   (SEAL)   _____
Witness   Buyer's Signature   Print Buyer's Name

_____   _____   (SEAL)   _____
Witness   Buyer's Signature   Print Buyer's Name

_____   _____   (SEAL)   _____
Witness   Seller's Signature   Print Seller's Name

_____   _____   (SEAL)   _____
Witness   Seller's Signature   Print Seller's Name

**STATEMENTS | ADDENDUM | RENTAL OR LEASED AGREEMENTS/CONTRACTS
| CONFIDENTIALITY AGREEMENT | DEPOSITS | LEGAL ADVICE AND DEPOSITS
– IF ANY INTEREST IS ACCRUED | INCORPORATION OF DOCUMENTS**

SCHEDULE _____   MLS® #:   DATE   Page of
ADDRESS:
LEGAL:
PID:
Further to the Contract of Purchase and Sale Dated
Made Between   as Buyers, and
                                                                          as Sellers and
covering the above mentioned property. The undersigned hereby agree as follows

RENTAL OR LEASED AGREEMENTS/CONTRACTS
*It is a fundamental term of this Contract of Purchase and Sale that if any item/service *[e.g. alarm system,
washer/dryer]* is under contract/monitor/lease/rental, the Sellers shall terminate and pay off such Contracts
in full prior to completion at no cost to the Buyers.
[Do you want to ask the Sellers to leave the e. g. non-operating alarm system in place]?

CONFIDENTIALITY AGREEMENT
*The Sellers and Buyers have signed separately in writing and prior to entering into this Contract of
Purchase and Sale a Confidentiality Agreement which is incorporated and forms part of this Contract of
Purchase and Sale and all parties warrant and guarantee to abide by the Confidentiality Agreement unless
otherwise mutually agreed to in writing by the Sellers and Buyers.

DEPOSITS | LEGAL ADVICE
*The *[Sellers/Buyers or the Sellers and Buyers]* hereby acknowledge that they have been advised to obtain
independent Legal/Professional advice before signing or accepting this Contract of Purchase and Sale with
respect to the arrangements for holding the deposit monies in this transaction.

DEPOSITS – IF ANY INTEREST IS ACCRUED
*The deposit is to be placed at interest and if any interest is accrued it will be for the benefit of the *[Sellers
or Buyers]*.

INCORPORATION OF DOCUMENTS
*Any and all documentation provided by the Sellers to the Buyers or the Buyers to the Sellers will be
attached to, incorporated and form part of this Contract of Purchase and Sale.

This Schedule is hereby incorporated and forms part of this Contract of Purchase and Sale entered into by
the parties as evidenced by their signatures below.
All parties have been afforded the opportunity and advised to SEEK INDEPENDENT LEGAL/PROFESSIONAL ADVICE before signing this
Agreement. Time shall remain of the essence. All other terms and conditions remain the same and in full force and effect.
Signed, Sealed and Delivered in the Presence of   **In Witness Whereof I have hereunder set my hand and seal**

_____   _____   _____
Witness   Buyer's Signature   Print Buyer's Name

_____   _____   _____
Witness   Buyer's Signature   Print Buyer's Name

_____   _____   _____
Witness   Seller's Signature   Print Seller's Name

_____   _____   _____
Witness   Seller's Signature   Print Seller's Name

Barbara Bell-Olsen

STATEMENTS | ADDENDUM | MEASUREMENTS/ROOM SIZES/SQUARE FOOTAGE/LOT SIZE/AGE |
NO GROWTH OR MANUFACTURE OF ILLEGAL SUBSTANCES AND OUTSTANDING ORDERS

SCHEDULE _____ MLS® #: DATE Page of
ADDRESS:
LEGAL:
PID:
Further to the Contract of Purchase and Sale Dated
Made Between   as Buyers, and
                                                                                                   as Sellers and
covering the above mentioned property. The undersigned hereby agree as follows

MEASUREMENTS/ROOM SIZES/SQUARE FOOTAGE/LOT SIZE/AGE *The Buyers have been advised that if further information or exact measurements, square footage and/or lot size is a concern, the property should be independently measured and the Buyers should also make their own investigations as to the age of the buildings/structures. The Buyers are advised to verify the above information and arrange for any independent measurements and/or investigations at the earliest possible opportunity and in any event prior to proceeding with this Contract of Purchase and Sale.

All parties have been afforded the opportunity and advised to obtain independent Legal/Professional advice *[and have waived their right to put a subject in the Contract of Purchase and Sale]* and accept and are satisfied with the above possible concerns.

NO GROWTH OR MANUFACTURE OF ILLEGAL SUBSTANCES
*The Sellers warrant and guarantee that during the time the Sellers have owned the property, the use of the land/property/buildings and structures thereon have not been for the growth or manufacture of any illegal substances and that to the best of the Sellers knowledge the use of the land/property/buildings and structures thereon have never been for the growth or manufacture of illegal substances. This warranty shall survive and not merge on the completion of this transaction.
The *[Sellers/Buyers or the Sellers and Buyers]* have been afforded the opportunity and advised to seek independent Legal/Professional advice.

OUTSTANDING ORDERS
*The Sellers warrant and guarantee there are no outstanding Work, Fire, Safety, Health or Environmental orders with any *[City/Municipal/Provincial/Governmental/Environmental]* Authorities/Regulators *[including the Strata Council, Strata Corporation and Property Management Companies if applicable]*.

This Schedule is hereby incorporated and forms part of this Contract of Purchase and Sale entered into by the parties as evidenced by their signatures below.
All parties have been afforded the opportunity and advised to SEEK INDEPENDENT LEGAL/PROFESSIONAL ADVICE before signing this Agreement. Time shall remain of the essence. All other terms and conditions remain the same and in full force and effect.
Signed, Sealed and Delivered in the Presence of   In Witness Whereof I have hereunder set my hand and seal

_____   _____   _____
Witness   Buyer's Signature   Print Buyer's Name

_____   _____   _____
Witness   Buyer's Signature   Print Buyer's Name

_____   _____   _____
Witness   Seller's Signature   Print Seller's Name

_____   _____   _____
Witness   Seller's Signature   Print Seller's Name

STATEMENTS | ADDENDUM | PLANS/PERMITS/DOCUMENTS/DRAWINGS WILL BE SUPPLIED BY THE SELLERS AND PROPERTY DISCLOSURE

SCHEDULE ____ MLS® #: DATE Page of
ADDRESS:
LEGAL:
PID:
Further to the Contract of Purchase and Sale Dated
Made Between as Buyers, and
as Sellers and
covering the above mentioned property. The undersigned hereby agree as follows

PLANS/PERMITS/DOCUMENTS/DRAWINGS WILL BE SUPPLIED BY THE SELLERS
*The Sellers warrant and guarantee to supply to the Buyers or the Buyers/Buyers' Agents/Representatives/ Brokerage within *[3 calendar]* days of acceptance of this Contract of Purchase and Sale by all parties, at no cost to the Buyers, any blueprints, building plans, drawings, and/or other plans/permits/documentation/ correspondence and warranties applicable to the land/property/buildings and structures that are in the Sellers' possession.
The Sellers agree to allow access for any of these parties if required including those already agreed to in the Access for All Trades Statement.

PROPERTY DISCLOSURE
*The Buyers have read, acknowledged and approved the attached Property Disclosure Statement which is incorporated into and forms part of this contract. The Buyers have been advised to seek independent Legal/ Professional advice prior to entering into this contract.

This Schedule is hereby incorporated and forms part of this Contract of Purchase and Sale entered into by the parties as evidenced by their signatures below.
All parties have been afforded the opportunity and advised to SEEK INDEPENDENT LEGAL/PROFESSIONAL ADVICE before signing this Agreement. Time shall remain of the essence. All other terms and conditions remain the same and in full force and effect.

Signed, Sealed and Delivered in the Presence of **In Witness Whereof I have hereunder set my hand and seal**

Witness	Buyer's Signature	SEAL	Print Buyer's Name
Witness	Buyer's Signature	SEAL	Print Buyer's Name
Witness	Seller's Signature	SEAL	Print Seller's Name
Witness	Seller's Signature	SEAL	Print Seller's Name

STATEMENTS | ADDENDUM | REFERRAL FEE DISCLOSURE | REMUNERATION DISCLOSURE | REGISTERING IN ANOTHER NAME AND RESIDENTS OF

SCHEDULE _____ MLS® #:   DATE   Page of
ADDRESS:
LEGAL:
PID:
Further to the Contract of Purchase and Sale Dated
Made Between   as Buyers, and
                                                         as Sellers and
covering the above mentioned property. The undersigned hereby agree as follows

REFERRAL FEE DISCLOSURE

*The *[Sellers/Buyers or the Sellers and Buyers]* acknowledge having received and signed a Disclosure of Referral Fees or *[other incentive/bonus points if applicable]* in accordance with the *[your Act or your Authorities/Regulators]* before the presentation of this Contract of Purchase and Sale.

REMUNERATION DISCLOSURE

*The *[Sellers/Buyers or the Sellers and Buyers]* acknowledge having received and signed a Disclosure of Remuneration in accordance with the *[your Act or your Authorities/ Regulators]* before the presentation of this Contract of Purchase and Sale. The *Sellers/Buyers or the Sellers and Buyers]* have been afforded the opportunity and advised to seek independent Legal/Professional advice.

REGISTERING IN ANOTHER NAME *[Do not use and/or Nominee]*

*For good and valuable consideration the Sellers and Buyers mutually agree that the Buyers can assign their rights under this Contract of Purchase and Sale and the agreement formed by its acceptance by all parties. The Buyers acknowledge and guarantee that such assignment would not in any way affect their obligations to complete the terms and conditions of this Contract of Purchase and Sale including their obligation to pay the purchase monies to the Sellers.
[Beware of the problems with the Financial Institutions].

RESIDENTS

*The Sellers hereby declare that they are Residents of [Canada] as defined under the Income Tax Act.

This Schedule is hereby incorporated and forms part of this Contract of Purchase and Sale entered into by the parties as evidenced by their signatures below.
All parties have been afforded the opportunity and advised to SEEK INDEPENDENT LEGAL/PROFESSIONAL ADVICE before signing this Agreement. Time shall remain of the essence. All other terms and conditions remain the same and in full force and effect.
Signed, Sealed and Delivered in the Presence of   **In Witness Whereof I have hereunder set my hand and seal**

_____   _____   _____
Witness   Buyer's Signature   Print Buyer's Name

_____   _____   _____
Witness   Buyer's Signature   Print Buyer's Name

_____   _____   _____
Witness   Seller's Signature   Print Seller's Name

_____   _____   _____
Witness   Seller's Signature   Print Seller's Name

STATEMENTS | ADDENDUM | RETURNING OF THE SELLERS' DOCUMENTS | SELLERS AGREE TO ALLOW TIME FOR BUYERS TO REMOVE SUBJECTS AND SELLERS HAVE DISCLOSED MATERIAL LATENT DEFECTS

SCHEDULE _____ MLS® #:   DATE   Page of

ADDRESS:

LEGAL:

PID:

Further to the Contract of Purchase and Sale Dated

Made Between   as Buyers, and

                                       as Sellers and

covering the above mentioned property. The undersigned hereby agree as follows

RETURNING OF THE SELLERS' DOCUMENTS

*In the event this transaction does not complete, the Buyers warrant and guarantee to return to the Sellers or the Sellers/Sellers' Agents/Representatives/Brokerage all documents/plans and Disclosures that the Buyers have received from the Sellers, within [3 calendar] days of the Sellers and Buyers signing an Unconditional Cancellation/Release.

SELLERS AGREE TO ALLOW TIME FOR BUYERS TO REMOVE SUBJECTS

*For good and valuable consideration of [One Dollar $1.00 or $_____] given by the Buyers and hereby acknowledged and received by the Sellers, the Sellers hereby warrant and guarantee that their acceptance of this offer will not be withdrawn or revoked prior to the date for all subjects to be removed. [Seal]

Time shall remain of the essence.

[Type the word [Seal] exactly as shown].

SELLERS HAVE DISCLOSED MATERIAL LATENT DEFECTS

*The Sellers warrant and guarantee that there are no Material Latent Defects as defined under their [Acts/ Legislation/Authorities/Regulators] and if there are they warrant and guarantee they have been disclosed separately in writing to the Buyers and the Buyers acknowledge receipt of and accept this Disclosure prior to entering into this Contract of Purchase and Sale of any and all Material Latent Defects regarding the condition and maintenance or any other items that could affect the land/property/buildings and structures including items designated lawfully or defined as Material Latent Defects [under your Acts/Legislation/ Authorities/Regulators].

The [Sellers/Buyers or the Sellers and Buyers] have been afforded the opportunity and advised to seek independent Legal/Professional advice]

[The disclosure, if any, will be attached to, incorporated and form part of this Contract of Purchase and Sale].

[This warranty shall survive and not merge on the completion of this transaction]?

This Schedule is hereby incorporated and forms part of this Contract of Purchase and Sale entered into by the parties as evidenced by their signatures below.

All parties have been afforded the opportunity and advised to SEEK INDEPENDENT LEGAL/PROFESSIONAL ADVICE before signing this Agreement. Time shall remain of the essence. All other terms and conditions remain the same and in full force and effect.

Signed, Sealed and Delivered in the Presence of   In Witness Whereof I have hereunder set my hand and seal

Witness	Buyer's Signature	Print Buyer's Name
Witness	Buyer's Signature	Print Buyer's Name
Witness	Seller's Signature	Print Seller's Name
Witness	Seller's Signature	Print Seller's Name

STATEMENTS | ADDENDUM | SELLERS HEREBY AUTHORIZE BUYERS TO OBTAIN DOCUMENTS AND INFORMATION | SELLERS WILL SIGN NECESSARY DOCUMENTATION AND ALLOW ACCESS AND SEPARATE DISCLOSURES | STATEMENTS

SCHEDULE _____ MLS® #:   DATE   Page of
ADDRESS:
LEGAL:
PID:
Further to the Contract of Purchase and Sale Dated
Made Between   as Buyers, and
                                                                    as Sellers and
covering the above mentioned property. The undersigned hereby agree as follows

SELLERS HEREBY AUTHORIZE BUYERS TO OBTAIN DOCUMENTS AND INFORMATION | [This puts the Buyers in the Sellers' Shoes]
*The Sellers hereby authorize the Buyers/Buyers' Agents/Representatives/Brokerage/Legal/Professional Representatives/Agents to view, inspect and obtain copies of any and all the records, correspondence, documents including but not limited to information that may be on record in the [your Authorities/ Regulators/Governmental Agencies including Strata Corporations/Councils/Property Managers if applicable] offices with respect to the said land/property/buildings/structures at no cost to the Sellers. The Sellers agree to allow access for any of these parties if required including those already agreed to in the Access for All Trades Statement.

SELLERS WILL SIGN NECESSARY DOCUMENTATION AND ALLOW ACCESS
*The Sellers warrant and guarantee to sign/authorize any applications/documentation required from any *[City/Municipal/Governmental/your Authorities/Regulators]* and/or any other trades/sources necessary at no cost to the Sellers for the Buyers/Buyers' Agents/Representatives/Brokerage to obtain any further information/documentation.
The Sellers agree to allow access for any of these parties if required including those already agreed to in the Access for All Trades Statement.

SEPARATE DISCLOSURES | STATEMENTS
*The Buyers/Sellers acknowledge having received and signed a [_____] *[prior to entering into this Contract of Purchase and Sale]* which is incorporated and forms part of this Contract of Purchase and Sale.
This Schedule is hereby incorporated and forms part of this Contract of Purchase and Sale entered into by the parties as evidenced by their signatures below.
All parties have been afforded the opportunity and advised to SEEK INDEPENDENT LEGAL/PROFESSIONAL ADVICE before signing this Agreement. Time shall remain of the essence. All other terms and conditions remain the same and in full force and effect.
Signed, Sealed and Delivered in the Presence of   **In Witness Whereof I have hereunder set my hand and seal**

_____   _____   _____
Witness   Buyer's Signature   Print Buyer's Name

_____   _____   _____
Witness   Buyer's Signature   Print Buyer's Name

_____   _____   _____
Witness   Seller's Signature   Print Seller's Name

_____   _____   _____
Witness   Seller's Signature   Print Seller's Name

STATEMENTS | ADDENDUM | SURVEY | TAXES | ACCOUNTING/PROFESSIONAL ADVICE | TAXES | PROPERTY ASSESSMENTS AND TAXES | PROPERTY TRANSFER TAX STATEMENT

SCHEDULE _____ MLS® #:   DATE   Page of
ADDRESS:
LEGAL:
PID:
Further to the Contract of Purchase and Sale Dated
Made Between   as Buyers, and
                                                as Sellers and
covering the above mentioned property. The undersigned hereby agree as follows

SURVEY

*If the Sellers have a Survey they will give it to the Buyers or the Buyers' Agents/Representatives/Brokerage within *[3 calendar]* days of acceptance of this Contract of Purchase and Sale by all parties and at no cost to the Buyers. The Sellers warrant and guarantee no additions, alterations or changes have been made including to the land/property/buildings and structures, fences and/or improvements since the date of the Survey *[which will be attached to, incorporated and form part of this contract]*.

TAXES | ACCOUNTING/PROFESSIONAL ADVICE

*The *[Sellers/Buyers or the Sellers and Buyers]* have been afforded the opportunity and advised to contact a Lawyer, Accountant or *[Canada Revenue Agency Office/Internal Revenue Service **or** your Authorities/ Regulators]* or other professionals with any questions/concerns regarding tax liability, exemptions, or the right to apply for any rebates if applicable. The tax and all rules/regulations related to real estate transactions can be complex and it is recommended to the *[Sellers/Buyers or the Sellers and Buyers]* that professional expert advice be obtained prior to entering into this Contract of Purchase and Sale.

TAXES | PROPERTY ASSESSMENTS

*The Sellers and Buyers accept and acknowledge that *[your Province/your Authorities/Regulators may]* have a system in place for assessment of properties and that the subject property may be reviewed and/or reassessed on an annual basis. The Sellers and Buyers warrant and guarantee that no claims will be made against the Sellers or Buyers' Agents/Representatives/Brokerages for any changes in the property tax as a result of any review or reassessment of the property.

TAXES | PROPERTY TRANSFER TAX STATEMENT

*The Buyers are aware of a _____% Property Transfer Tax up to $_____ of the purchase price and _____% on the balance.

This Schedule is hereby incorporated and forms part of this Contract of Purchase and Sale entered into by the parties as evidenced by their signatures below.

All parties have been afforded the opportunity and advised to SEEK INDEPENDENT LEGAL/PROFESSIONAL ADVICE before signing this Agreement. Time shall remain of the essence. All other terms and conditions remain the same and in full force and effect.

Signed, Sealed and Delivered in the Presence of   In Witness Whereof I have hereunder set my hand and seal

_____   _____   SEAL   _____
Witness   Buyer's Signature   Print Buyer's Name

_____   _____   SEAL   _____
Witness   Buyer's Signature   Print Buyer's Name

_____   _____   SEAL   _____
Witness   Seller's Signature   Print Seller's Name

_____   _____   SEAL   _____
Witness   Seller's Signature   Print Seller's Name

STATEMENTS | ADDENDUM | TITLE INSURANCE | TITLE SEARCH

SCHEDULE _____ MLS® #:   DATE   Page of
ADDRESS:
LEGAL:
PID:
Further to the Contract of Purchase and Sale Dated
Made Between   as Buyers, and
                                                            as Sellers and
covering the above mentioned property. The undersigned hereby agree as follows

TITLE INSURANCE

*The Buyers have been advised to research Title Insurance prior to completion of this Contract of Purchase and Sale and it is solely their option whether or not to purchase the same. It is recommended that the Buyers may still want to obtain a Survey and have been advised to research both Title Insurance and Survey information prior to entering into this Contract of Purchase and Sale.

TITLE SEARCH

*The Buyers have read, acknowledged and accepted the Title Search. In addition to any encumbrances referred to in the preprinted wording in this Contract of Purchase and Sale, the Buyers have read, acknowledge and accept that on Completion/Registration the Buyers will receive title containing:
1. Any non-financial charges, and
2. Any financial charges payable by a utility on its right of way/restrictive covenant/easement or other interest set out in the copy of the Title Search results that are attached, form part of and are incorporated in this Contract of Purchase and Sale and any financial charges payable by a utility on its right of way, restrictive covenant, easement, statutory rights-of-way, building schemes or other interest set out in the copy of the Title Search results. The Buyers are aware that these run with the land and will remain on title.

The Buyers are aware that these charges may affect their use or value of the property and have been advised to seek independent Legal/Professional advice with respect to all charges prior to entering into this Contract of Purchase and Sale.

Continued ...

This Schedule is hereby incorporated and forms part of this Contract of Purchase and Sale entered into by the parties as evidenced by their signatures below.

All parties have been afforded the opportunity and advised to SEEK INDEPENDENT LEGAL/PROFESSIONAL ADVICE before signing this Agreement. Time shall remain of the essence. All other terms and conditions remain the same and in full force and effect.

Signed, Sealed and Delivered in the Presence of   **In Witness Whereof I have hereunder set my hand and seal**

_____   _____   _____
Witness   Buyer's Signature   Print Buyer's Name

_____   _____   _____
Witness   Buyer's Signature   Print Buyer's Name

_____   _____   _____
Witness   Seller's Signature   Print Seller's Name

_____   _____   _____
Witness   Seller's Signature   Print Seller's Name

STATEMENTS | ADDENDUM | WAIVER OF SUBJECTS

SCHEDULE _____ MLS® #:   DATE   Page of
ADDRESS:
LEGAL:
PID:
Further to the Contract of Purchase and Sale Dated
Made Between   as Buyers, and
                                                       as Sellers and
covering the above mentioned property. The undersigned hereby agree as follows

TITLE SEARCH Continued ...

Do you want to include this?

Charge in Favour Of   **Charge #**

[_____ # _____]
[_____ # _____]
[_____ # _____]

Do you want to include this?

The Sellers warrant and guarantee to provide to the Buyers or the Buyers' Agents/Representatives/ Brokerage *[at no cost to the Buyers]*, within *[3 calendar days]* of acceptance of this Contract of Purchase and Sale by all parties, a full copy/explanation of any and all non-financial legal notations including but not limited to Covenants, Building Schemes, Easements, Restrictive Covenants and any unknown/unclear charges showing on the Title [Surface] Search.

WAIVER OF SUBJECTS

* If the Buyers are proceeding with this Contract of Purchase and Sale after having the opportunity to perform their due diligence including the services of Legal/Professional Representatives and the Buyers choose to waive any/all of their subjects instead of fulfilling/removing their beneficial subjects, *[the Buyers hereby warrant and guarantee to execute a waiver at the time of completion. This will be handled by the Lawyers/Notaries at the time of conveyance]. [The attached 'Confirm your Advice' is incorporated and forms part of this Contract of Purchase and Sale]*.

This Schedule is hereby incorporated and forms part of this Contract of Purchase and Sale entered into by the parties as evidenced by their signatures below.

All parties have been afforded the opportunity and advised to SEEK INDEPENDENT LEGAL/PROFESSIONAL ADVICE before signing this Agreement. Time shall remain of the essence. All other terms and conditions remain the same and in full force and effect.

Signed, Sealed and Delivered in the Presence of   **In Witness Whereof I have hereunder set my hand and seal**

_____   _____   _____
Witness   Buyer's Signature   Print Buyer's Name

_____   _____   _____
Witness   Buyer's Signature   Print Buyer's Name

_____   _____   _____
Witness   Seller's Signature   Print Seller's Name

_____   _____   _____
Witness   Seller's Signature   Print Seller's Name

SUBJECTS IN MOST CONTRACTS | THE FAMOUS FIVE | INDEX

1. Financing

- Finalization of the Preapproved Mortgage

- Satisfactory Financing

- Specific Details

- Can the Sellers Clear the Title?

2. Insurance

- Fire Property Insurance | Residential

- Strata Property

3. Inspection

- Residential

- Strata

4. Property Disclosure Statement

5. Title Search

SUBJECTS | FINALIZATION OF THE PREAPPROVED MORTGAGE
SUBJECTS | SATISFACTORY FINANCING

SCHEDULE _____ MLS® #:   DATE   Page of
ADDRESS:
LEGAL:
PID:
Further to the Contract of Purchase and Sale Dated
Made Between   as Buyers, and
                                                    as Sellers and
covering the above mentioned property. The undersigned hereby agree as follows
SUBJECT
FINANCING | FINALIZATION OF THE PREAPPROVED MORTGAGE
This Contract of Purchase and Sale is subject to finalization of the preapproved mortgage *[in the amount of*
$_____] on or before *[date]*.
This subject is for the sole benefit of the Buyers.
*For good and valuable consideration of *[One Dollar $1.00 or $_____]* given by the Buyers and
hereby acknowledged and received by the Sellers, the Sellers hereby warrant and guarantee that their
acceptance of this offer will not be withdrawn or revoked prior to the date for all subjects to be removed. [Seal]
Time shall remain of the essence.
[Type the word [Seal] exactly as shown].

OR

SUBJECT
FINANCING | SATISFACTORY FINANCING
This Contract of Purchase and Sale is subject to the Buyers obtaining satisfactory financing on or before
[date].
This subject is for the sole benefit of the Buyers.
*For good and valuable consideration of *[One Dollar $1.00 or $_____]* given by the Buyers and hereby
acknowledged and received by the Sellers, the Sellers hereby warrant and guarantee that their acceptance of this
offer will not be withdrawn or revoked prior to the date for all subjects to be removed. [Seal]
Time shall remain of the essence.
[Type the word [Seal] exactly as shown].
All parties have been afforded the opportunity and advised to SEEK INDEPENDENT LEGAL/PROFESSIONAL ADVICE before signing this
Agreement. Time shall remain of the essence. All other terms and conditions remain the same and in full force and effect.
Signed, Sealed and Delivered in the Presence of   In Witness Whereof I have hereunder set my hand and seal

_____   _____   _____
Witness   Buyer's Signature   Print Buyer's Name

_____   _____   _____
Witness   Buyer's Signature   Print Buyer's Name

_____   _____   _____
Witness   Seller's Signature   Print Seller's Name

_____   _____   _____
Witness   Seller's Signature   Print Seller's Name

Barbara Bell-Olsen

SUBJECTS | SPECIFIC DETAILS

SCHEDULE _____ MLS® #:   DATE   Page of
ADDRESS:
LEGAL:
PID:
Further to the Contract of Purchase and Sale Dated
Made Between   as Buyers, and
                                                    as Sellers and
covering the above mentioned property. The undersigned hereby agree as follows

SUBJECT
FINANCING | SPECIFIC DETAILS

This Contract of Purchase and Sale is subject to a new first mortgage being made available
to the Buyer by _____, in the amount of $_____ at an interest rate
not to exceed _____% per annum calculated half-yearly, not in advance, with
a _____ - year amortization period, _____ - year term and
repayable in blended payments of approximately $_____ per month including
principal and interest [plus 1/12 of the annual taxes, if required by the mortgagee].
This subject is for the sole benefit of the Buyers.

All parties have been afforded the opportunity and advised to SEEK INDEPENDENT LEGAL/PROFESSIONAL ADVICE before signing this
Agreement. Time shall remain of the essence. All other terms and conditions remain the same and in full force and effect.
Signed, Sealed and Delivered in the Presence of   **In Witness Whereof I have hereunder set my hand and seal**

_____   _____   _____
Witness   Buyer's Signature   Print Buyer's Name

_____   _____   _____
Witness   Buyer's Signature   Print Buyer's Name

_____   _____   _____
Witness   Seller's Signature   Print Seller's Name

_____   _____   _____
Witness   Seller's Signature   Print Seller's Name

SUBJECTS | CAN THE SELLERS CLEAR THE TITLE?

SCHEDULE _____ MLS® #:   DATE   Page of
ADDRESS:
LEGAL:
PID:
Further to the Contract of Purchase and Sale Dated
Made Between   as Buyers, and
                                                       as Sellers and
covering the above mentioned property. The undersigned hereby agree as follows
SUBJECT
CAN THE SELLERS CLEAR THE TITLE?
This Contract of Purchase and Sale is subject to the Sellers' confirmation and satisfaction with the arrangement of their financial affairs, on or *[date]*, which enable the Sellers to proceed with this sale. This subject is for the sole benefit of the Sellers.
For good and valuable consideration of *[One Dollar $1.00 or $_____]* given by the **Sellers** and hereby acknowledged and received by the **Buyers**, the **Buyers** hereby warrant and guarantee that their acceptance of this offer will not be withdrawn or revoked prior to the date for all subjects to be removed. [Seal]
Time shall remain of the essence.
[Type the word [Seal] exactly as shown].
OR
The Sellers accept and are aware that this property is subject to any/all registered encumbrances and that combined with the obligation for the Sellers to pay commissions and other closing costs, may or do exceed the proceeds of sale from this transaction. This Contract of Purchase and Sale is subject to the Sellers on or before *[date]*, obtaining the written approval of all Charges/Mortgagees and other registered encumbrances as to the final acceptance of this Contract of Purchase and Sale and their agreement to discharge their encumbrances without payment in the aggregate of more than the available proceeds from this transaction.
This subject is for the sole benefit of the Sellers.
For good and valuable consideration of *[One Dollar $1.00 or $_____]* given by the **Sellers** and hereby acknowledged and received by the **Buyers**, the **Buyers** hereby warrant and guarantee that their acceptance of this offer will not be withdrawn or revoked prior to the date for all subjects to be removed. [Seal]
Time shall remain of the essence.
[Type the word [Seal] exactly as shown].
All parties have been afforded the opportunity and advised to SEEK INDEPENDENT LEGAL/PROFESSIONAL ADVICE before signing this Agreement. Time shall remain of the essence. All other terms and conditions remain the same and in full force and effect.
Signed, Sealed and Delivered in the Presence of   **In Witness Whereof I have hereunder set my hand and seal**

_____   _____   _____
Witness   Buyer's Signature   Print Buyer's Name

_____   _____   _____
Witness   Buyer's Signature   Print Buyer's Name

_____   _____   _____
Witness   Seller's Signature   Print Seller's Name

_____   _____   _____
Witness   Seller's Signature   Print Seller's Name

SUBJECTS | FIRE PROPERTY INSURANCE | RESIDENTIAL

SCHEDULE _____ MLS® #: DATE Page of
ADDRESS:
LEGAL:
PID:
Further to the Contract of Purchase and Sale Dated
Made Between   as Buyers, and
                                                      as Sellers and
covering the above mentioned property. The undersigned hereby agree as follows

SUBJECT

FIRE PROPERTY INSURANCE | Residential

This Contract of Purchase and Sale is subject to the Buyers at their expense confirming that there are no pre-existing issues or conditions that would prevent the Buyers from obtaining insurance coverage including but not limited to content, liability, specified perils on or before *[date]*. This subject is for the sole benefit of the Buyer.

The Sellers agree to allow access for any of these parties if required including those already agreed to in the Access for All Trades Statement.

Do you want to include this?

[The Sellers warrant and guarantee to give a copy of their current Insurance Policy to the Buyers or the Buyers' Agents/Representatives/Brokerage within [3] calendar days of acceptance of this Contract of Purchase and Sale by all parties and at no cost to the Buyers.]

The Buyers have been advised to seek independent Legal/Insurance/Professional advice.

*For good and valuable consideration of *[One Dollar $1.00 or $_____]* given by the Buyers and hereby acknowledged and received by the Sellers, the Sellers hereby warrant and guarantee that their acceptance of this offer will not be withdrawn or revoked prior to the date for all subjects to be removed. [Seal]

Time shall remain of the essence.

[Type the word [Seal] exactly as shown].

All parties have been afforded the opportunity and advised to SEEK INDEPENDENT LEGAL/PROFESSIONAL ADVICE before signing this Agreement. Time shall remain of the essence. All other terms and conditions remain the same and in full force and effect.

Signed, Sealed and Delivered in the Presence of   **In Witness Whereof I have hereunder set my hand and seal**

_____   _____   🔘SEAL _____
Witness   Buyer's Signature   Print Buyer's Name

_____   _____   🔘SEAL _____
Witness   Buyer's Signature   Print Buyer's Name

_____   _____   🔘SEAL _____
Witness   Seller's Signature   Print Seller's Name

_____   _____   🔘SEAL _____
Witness   Seller's Signature   Print Seller's Name

SUBJECTS | STRATA | INSURANCE SUBJECTS | ADDENDUM

SCHEDULE _____ MLS® #: DATE Page of
ADDRESS:
LEGAL:
PID:
Further to the Contract of Purchase and Sale Dated
Made Between   as Buyers, and
                                                                                 as Sellers and
covering the above mentioned property. The undersigned hereby agree as follows

Subject
Insurance | Strata Property
Summary of Coverage of Insurance and [*Condominium Homeowner, Landlord or Tenants Insurance Policy]
This Contract of Purchase and Sale is subject to the Buyers receiving and approving at no cost to the Sellers, a copy of the Insurance Policy and/or 'Summary of Coverage of Insurance' for the Owners of Strata Plan *[Name/Number]* and subject to the Buyers confirming the availability of insurance coverage including content, liability, specified perils *[and_____]* on or before *[date]*.
AND/OR [I personally would include both these subjects.]
This Contract of Purchase and Sale is subject to the Buyers confirming that there are no pre-existing issues or conditions that would prevent the buyers from obtaining insurance coverage including content, liability, specified perils *[and_____]* on or before *[date]*.
This condition is for the sole benefit of the Buyer.
Do you want to include this?
[The Sellers warrant and guarantee to give a copy of their current Insurance Policy to the Buyers or the Buyers' Agents/Representatives/Brokerage within [3] calendar days of acceptance of this Contract of Purchase and Sale by all parties and at no cost to the Buyers.]

The Buyers have been advised to seek independent Legal/Insurance/Professional advice.
The Sellers agree to allow access for any of these parties if required including those already agreed to in the Access for All Trades Statement.
*For good and valuable consideration of *[One Dollar $1.00 or $_____]* given by the Buyers and hereby acknowledged and received by the Sellers, the Sellers hereby warrant and guarantee that their acceptance of this offer will not be withdrawn or revoked prior to the date for all subjects to be removed.
[Seal]
Time shall remain of the essence.
[Type the word [Seal] exactly as shown].
All parties have been afforded the opportunity and advised to SEEK INDEPENDENT LEGAL/PROFESSIONAL ADVICE before signing this Agreement. Time shall remain of the essence. All other terms and conditions remain the same and in full force and effect.
Signed, Sealed and Delivered in the Presence of   **In Witness Whereof I have hereunder set my hand and seal**

_____   _____   _____
Witness   Buyer's Signature   Print Buyer's Name

_____   _____   _____
Witness   Buyer's Signature   Print Buyer's Name

_____   _____   _____
Witness   Seller's Signature   Print Seller's Name

_____   _____   _____
Witness   Seller's Signature   Print Seller's Name

SUBJECTS | INSPECTION OF THE PROPERTY | RESIDENTIAL

SCHEDULE _____ MLS® #:   DATE   Page of
ADDRESS:
LEGAL:
PID:
Further to the Contract of Purchase and Sale Dated
Made Between   as Buyers, and
                                                      as Sellers and
covering the above mentioned property. The undersigned hereby agree as follows

SUBJECT
INSPECTION OF THE PROPERTY | RESIDENTIAL
This Contract of Purchase and Sale is subject to the Buyers, on or before [date], at the Buyers' expense, obtaining and approving an inspection report [or professional inspection] against any defects [whose cumulative cost of repair exceeds $_____ and] which reasonably may adversely affect the property's use or value.
This subject is for the sole benefit of the Buyers.
The Sellers agree to allow access for any of these parties if required including those already agreed to in the Access for All Trades Statement.
*For good and valuable consideration of *[One Dollar $1.00 or $_____]* given by the Buyers and hereby acknowledged and received by the Sellers, the Sellers hereby warrant and guarantee that their acceptance of this offer will not be withdrawn or revoked prior to the date for all subjects to be removed. [Seal]
Time shall remain of the essence.
[Type the word [Seal] exactly as shown.]

All parties have been afforded the opportunity and advised to SEEK INDEPENDENT LEGAL/PROFESSIONAL ADVICE before signing this Agreement. Time shall remain of the essence. All other terms and conditions remain the same and in full force and effect.
Signed, Sealed and Delivered in the Presence of   **In Witness Whereof I have hereunder set my hand and seal**

_____   _____   _____
Witness   Buyer's Signature   Print Buyer's Name

_____   _____   _____
Witness   Buyer's Signature   Print Buyer's Name

_____   _____   _____
Witness   Seller's Signature   Print Seller's Name

_____   _____   _____
Witness   Seller's Signature   Print Seller's Name

SUBJECTS | STRATA | SUBJECT | ADDENDUM | INSPECTIONS OF THE PROPERTY

SCHEDULE _____   MLS® #:   DATE   Page of
ADDRESS:
LEGAL:
PID:
Further to the Contract of Purchase and Sale Dated
Made Between   as Buyers, and
                                                            as Sellers and
covering the above mentioned property. The undersigned hereby agree as follows
Subject
Inspections of the Property | Strata
This Contract of Purchase and Sale is subject to the Buyers, on or before *[date]*, at the Buyers' expense, obtaining and approving an inspection report *[or professional inspection]* against any defects *[whose cumulative cost of repair exceeds $ and]* which reasonably may adversely affect the property's use or value.
The Sellers agree to allow access for any of these parties if required including those already agreed to in the Access for All Trades Statement.
This subject is for the sole benefit of the Buyers.

The Sellers/Sellers' Agents/Representatives/Brokerage warrant and guarantee to arrange, on reasonable notice, for the purposes of inspection, access to the suite and common areas such as, but not limited to, the roof, the electrical room, boiler or furnace room, parking areas, storage areas and recreational areas, at no cost to the Buyers/Buyers' Agents/Representatives/Brokerage.

*For good and valuable consideration of *[One Dollar $1.00 or $_____]* given by the Buyers and hereby acknowledged and received by the Sellers, the Sellers hereby warrant and guarantee that their acceptance of this offer will not be withdrawn or revoked prior to the date for all subjects to be removed.
[Seal]
Time shall remain of the essence.
[Type the word [Seal] exactly as shown.]

[Remember you cannot give out copies of the Report without written consent of the Inspector and/or Buyers/ Sellers.]

All parties have been afforded the opportunity and advised to SEEK INDEPENDENT LEGAL/PROFESSIONAL ADVICE before signing this Agreement. Time shall remain of the essence. All other terms and conditions remain the same and in full force and effect.
Signed, Sealed and Delivered in the Presence of   **In Witness Whereof I have hereunder set my hand and seal**

_____	_____	_____
Witness	Buyer's Signature	Print Buyer's Name
_____	_____	_____
Witness	Buyer's Signature	Print Buyer's Name
_____	_____	_____
Witness	Seller's Signature	Print Seller's Name
_____	_____	_____
Witness	Seller's Signature	Print Seller's Name

SUBJECTS | REMOVED/FULFILLED OR WAIVED | SAMPLE ADDENDUM

SCHEDULE _____ MLS® #:   DATE   Page of
ADDRESS:
LEGAL:
PID:
Further to the Contract of Purchase and Sale Dated
Made Between   as Buyers, and
                                                                                 as Sellers and
covering the above mentioned property. The undersigned hereby agree as follows

To **REMOVE** the following subjects, namely **OR**
To **FULFILL** the following subjects, namely:

This Contract of Purchase and Sale is subject to finalization of the preapproved mortgage *[in the amount of*
$_____] on or before [date].
This subject is for the sole benefit of the Buyers.

This Contract of Purchase and Sale is subject to the Buyers, on or before [date], at the Buyers' expense,
obtaining and approving an inspection report [or professional inspection] against any defects [whose
cumulative cost of repair exceeds $_____ and] which reasonably may adversely affect the
property's use or value.
This subject is for the sole benefit of the Buyers.

To **WAIVE** the following subjects, namely:
This Contract of Purchase and Sale is subject to the Buyers at their expense confirming that there are
no pre-existing issues or conditions that would prevent the Buyers from obtaining insurance coverage
including but not limited to content, liability, specified perils on or before *[date]*. This subject is for the sole
benefit of the Buyer.

.

All parties have been afforded the opportunity and advised to SEEK INDEPENDENT LEGAL/PROFESSIONAL ADVICE before signing this
Agreement. Time shall remain of the essence. All other terms and conditions remain the same and in full force and effect.
Signed, Sealed and Delivered in the Presence of   **In Witness Whereof I have hereunder set my hand and seal**

Witness	Buyer's Signature	Print Buyer's Name
Witness	Buyer's Signature	Print Buyer's Name
Witness	Seller's Signature	Print Seller's Name
Witness	Seller's Signature	Print Seller's Name

TENANTS | ASKING THE TENANTS TO VACATE | ONE MONTH'S FREE RENT | STATEMENTS AND IF ANY VACATE NOT TO RE-RENT

SCHEDULE _____ MLS® #:   DATE   Page of
ADDRESS:
LEGAL:
PID:
Further to the Contract of Purchase and Sale Dated
Made Between   as Buyers, and
                                                                  as Sellers and
covering the above mentioned property. The undersigned hereby agree as follows
Statement
Asking the Tenants to Vacate *[3 Statements]*
1. The Sellers will give legal notice to the Tenants to vacate the premises, but only if the Sellers receive the appropriate written request from the Buyers to give such notice in accordance with the requirements of the *[Residential Tenancy Act or the name of your Act]*. The Sellers warrant and guarantee to give a copy of the legal notice served to the tenants to the Buyers or the Buyers' Agents/Representatives/Brokerage *[within 24 hours]* of such notice being officially served to the tenants.

2. If the Sellers/Landlord do not give the tenants the one month's free rent, the Sellers/Landlord warrant and guarantee that they will pay the tenants on or before *[1:00 p.m.]* on the effective date of the notice, any and all costs required to vacate the tenants under the *[Residential Tenancy Act or the name of your Act]*.

3. If any of the tenants give notice to vacate or do vacate prior to completion, the Sellers/Landlord will immediately notify the Buyers in writing including giving a copy of any notices received to the Buyers/ Buyers' Agents/Representatives/Brokerage. The Sellers/Landlord also warrant and guarantee *[unless otherwise agreed to in writing]*, not to re-rent the suite/house/vacancies including any other vacancies *[if applicable]* including the garage/carport/shed/lockers *[if applicable]*.
Is this already included in your Statements pages?
*Any and all documentation provided by the Sellers to the Buyers or the Buyers to the Sellers will be attached to, incorporated and form part of this Contract of Purchase and Sale.

If any of the tenants vacate prior to completion, the Sellers warrant not to re-rent the suite *[garage/ carport/shed/locker if applicable]*.
All parties have been afforded the opportunity and advised to SEEK INDEPENDENT LEGAL/PROFESSIONAL ADVICE before signing this Agreement. Time shall remain of the essence. All other terms and conditions remain the same and in full force and effect.
Signed, Sealed and Delivered in the Presence of   In Witness Whereof I have hereunder set my hand and seal

Witness	Buyer's Signature	Print Buyer's Name
Witness	Buyer's Signature	Print Buyer's Name
Witness	Seller's Signature	Print Seller's Name
Witness	Seller's Signature	Print Seller's Name

TENANTS | INFORMATION ABOUT THE TENANTS | STATEMENT | ADDENDUM

SCHEDULE _____ MLS® #:   DATE   Page of
ADDRESS:
LEGAL:
PID:
Further to the Contract of Purchase and Sale Dated
Made Between   as Buyers, and
                                                               as Sellers and
covering the above mentioned property. The undersigned hereby agree as follows
Statement | Information about the Tenants
BASEMENT TENANTS
The Seller warrants the tenant is *[_____name_____]* who occupies *[__the main floor/ basement/upper floor or __]*; the monthly rent is *[$_____]* including *[list utilities etc.]*; payable on *[date]*; a security deposit of *[$_____]* was taken on *[date]*; and the last rental increase was *[date]*. The Seller warrants the Tenancy is month to month. Any damage/security deposit and any pet deposit taken will be adjusted between the parties on closing.

MAIN FLOOR TENANTS
The Seller warrants the tenant is *[_____name_____]* who occupies *[__the main floor/ basement/upper floor or __]*; the monthly rent is *[$_____]* including *[list utilities etc.]*; payable on *[date]*; a security deposit of *[$_____]* was taken on *[date]*; and the last rental increase was *[date]*. The Seller warrants the Tenancy is month to month. Any damage/security deposit and any pet deposit taken will be adjusted between the parties on closing.

UPPER FLOOR TENANTS
The Seller warrants the tenant is *[_____name_____]* who occupies *[__the main floor/ basement/upper floor or __]*; the monthly rent is *[$_____]* including *[list utilities etc.]*; payable on *[date]*; a security deposit of *[$_____]* was taken on *[date]*; and the last rental increase was *[date]*. The Seller warrants the Tenancy is month to month. Any damage/security deposit and any pet deposit taken will be adjusted between the parties on closing.
The Sellers/Sellers' Representative/Brokerage will give a copy of any and all written tenancy agreements to the Buyers/Buyers' Representative/Brokerage within *[24 hours]* of acceptance of this Contract by all parties.

Is this already included in your Statements pages?
*Any and all documentation provided by the Sellers to the Buyers or the Buyers to the Sellers will be attached to, incorporated and form part of this Contract of Purchase and Sale.

All parties have been afforded the opportunity and advised to SEEK INDEPENDENT LEGAL/PROFESSIONAL ADVICE before signing this Agreement. Time shall remain of the essence. All other terms and conditions remain the same and in full force and effect.
Signed, Sealed and Delivered in the Presence of   **In Witness Whereof I have hereunder set my hand and seal**

_____	_____	_____
Witness	Buyer's Signature	Print Buyer's Name
_____	_____	_____
Witness	Buyer's Signature	Print Buyer's Name
_____	_____	_____
Witness	Seller's Signature	Print Seller's Name
_____	_____	_____
Witness	Seller's Signature	Print Seller's Name

TENANTS | NOTICE TO TENANTS FOR A SHOWING

Date _____

To Whom It May Concern/or _____

Tenants' Names

This notice is to advise the Tenants at _____

Address

that a showing of your residences will be held on _____

Date

at _____ a.m. p.m. or between the hours of _____.

The reason for the showing is to show prospective or interested Buyers the residences/property.

This notice has been given in accordance with the *Residential Tenancy Act*. If there are any questions, please contact us at your earliest convenience.

Real Estate Agents/Reps _____

Names and Contact Info

Of _____

Brokerage name

_____

Address	City	Province	Postal Code	Phone Number

Signature _____

Real Estate Agents/Reps

Signature: _____

Real Estate Agents/Reps

Your Authorities/Legislators may have a prescribed form you must use

TENANTS | NOTICE TO TENANTS FOR MULTIPLE SHOWINGS

Date _____

To Whom It May Concern/or _____
Tenants' Names

This notice is to advise the Tenants at _____
Address

that a showing of your residences/property will be held on the following dates and times in order to show prospective or interested Buyers.

This notice has been given in accordance with the *Residential Tenancy Act.* If there are any questions, please contact us at your earliest convenience.

Real Estate Agents/Reps _____
Names and Contact Info

Of _____
Brokerage name

_____

| Address | City | Province | Postal Code | Phone Number |

Signature _____
Real Estate Agents/Reps

Signature: _____
Real Estate Agents/Reps

DAY	DATE	TIMES	REASON

_____To show prospective/interested Buyers

_____To show prospective/interested Buyers

_____To show prospective/interested Buyers

_____To show prospective/interested Buyers

_____To show prospective/interested Buyers

_____To show prospective/interested Buyers

_____To show prospective/interested Buyers

_____To show prospective/interested Buyers

_____To show prospective/interested Buyers

_____To show prospective/interested Buyers

_____To show prospective/interested Buyers

_____To show prospective/interested Buyers

Your Authorities/Legislators may have a prescribed form you must use

THANK YOU FOR YOUR OFFER OR COUNTER-OFFER

Please Print Clearly

Re Property _____
Address   City   Province   Postal Code

Legal_____PID #_____

Name of Sellers _____

Name of Sellers _____

Name of Buyers _____

Name of Buyers _____

Listing Agents/Reps _____
Agents and Contact Info

Listing Brokerage_____
Brokerage name and Contact Info

Buyers' Agents/Reps _____
Agents and Contact Info

Buyers' Brokerage _____
Brokerage Name and Contact Info

Thank you very much for your offer or counter-offer.

We confirm that your offer/counter-offer was presented at _____a.m. / p.m.
On _____20_____ and was not accepted or countered back.
        Day   Month   Year

Comments *[if any]* _____

_____

_____

In Witness Whereof I have hereunder set my hand and seal   **Signed, Sealed and Delivered in the Presence of**

(SEAL) _____
        Seller's or Buyer's Signature   Witness   Date

(SEAL) _____
        Seller's or Buyer's Signature   Witness   Date

(SEAL) _____
        Seller's or Buyer's Signature   Witness   Date

(SEAL) _____
        Seller's or Buyer's Signature   Witness   Date

Your Authorities/Legislators may have a prescribed form you must use

UNAUTHORIZED ACCOMMODATIONS/RENOVATIONS | CONSENT TO ADVERTISE

We_____

Name of Sellers

Owners of_____

Property Address

Legal: _____ PID #_____

Authorize our Real Estate Agents/Reps _____

Names and Contact Info

Of _____

Brokerage name

_____

| Address | City | Province | Postal Code | Phone Number |

to advertise the unauthorized or illegal accommodations or renovations that exist in my property. This distribution may also include via electronic means.

We acknowledge that such advertising may result in Civic/Municipal/Governmental Officials taking action to require us to remove, alter, upgrade or close the unauthorized or illegal accommodations or renovations.

We hereby release_____

Agents/Reps

and_____

Brokerage

from any liability with regard to the said advertising and we acknowledge that you will advise prospective Buyers the consequences of such ownership including the potential loss of income from the said unauthorized or illegal accommodation or renovations.

We also acknowledge that under the Legislation the above are considered Material Latent Defects and written disclosure of all known Material Latent Defects <u>must be provided in writing to the Buyers before there is an accepted offer</u>. Timing of the disclosure is critical.

The Sellers have been afforded the opportunity and advised to SEEK INDEPENDENT LEGAL/ PROFESSIONAL ADVICE before signing this consent and authorization to advertise unauthorized accommodations/renovations.

In Witness Whereof I have hereunder set my hand and seal Signed, Sealed and Delivered in the Presence of

_____   _____
Seller's Signature   Witness

Date_____

_____   _____
Seller's Signature   Witness

Date_____

[A copy must be given to all parties, your Brokerage and a copy kept in your files]

Your Authorities/Legislators may have a prescribed form you must use

INDEX